Don't Feed the Ducks...

Inspire your people, create a brilliant business

650.1

Published by Accent Press Ltd – 2010

ISBN 9781907016523

Copyright © Liam O'Connell 2007

X000 000 042 8502

A000 000 001 5497

Dedication

This book is dedicated to

My mom

Roy

And Sue

Without you it would not have been possible

xxxx

Also by Liam O'Connell

Published by Accent Press

My Fire's Gone Out!

My Fire's Gone Out! is a simple, funny and yet
profound story about coping with change.
The fire is a metaphor for what is really important
to you in your life or your work.
In this fast-paced modern world we live in, we are
faced with many challenges and complex choices.
Sometimes our personal fire can go out and this book can
help you get that spark back
to relight your fire!
Read it in an hour and change your life for good!

ISBN 9781907016516

Contents

Foreword

It was at a conference in Harrogate in 2003 that I first came across Liam O'Connell in the 'innovation theatre' – five speakers with ten minutes each.

Ten minutes isn't long, but he really seized the moment and took advantage of his opportunity. So did I. Straight after the session I fixed up for Liam to speak at our first ever staff conference. It was just as well because, on the day, he was what made it worth attending for our staff.

Liam has since become a good friend, one that I always feel better for talking to. He's always so positive. I've seen him perform at many events across the UK and although he has continued to develop himself and his approach, the impact is always the same. If you're reading this book as a result of seeing Liam you'll know what I mean. If you haven't, you'll enjoy the book just as much but do try to catch Liam at an event some time.

It's the sort of book that will make you think about your own approach and that of your colleagues and your organisation. It's about transformation and attitude, and the positive people whose stories are told here will inspire you – not just the first time you read it. It's a book that you'll keep returning to – we all need a 'prod' sometimes, a reminder of what it's really about. We also need to have a bit of fun along the way.

The great thing is that, if you're able to harness just some of the passion from these pages and embed it into your business, what a difference you'll make for your customers. Read on, and don't ever let Liam catch you feeding the ducks again, at least not in the workplace!

Paul Diggory
President, Chartered Institute of Housing 2007–08
Chief Executive, North Wales Housing Association

Acknowledgements

Many thanks to everybody who has helped so much

David Birkett
Ron Dougan
Jim Morrison
The Bridge Group
Cragrats, Dave Bradley, Dave Hill, Mark Greenop, Leah
Julia Peckham – 'J' Steve, Daisy, Martha
The Wrekin Housing Trust – John Broadhead, Jane Brookes,
Francis Best, Beverley, Catherine, Sara
Linda, Darren and everybody at the University of Essex
Linda and Don
Phil, Sal
Paul Diggory
Mark Gardner
Lindsey Williams, Nicky Townsend
Geoff, Ni, Helen, Nicky and Paul
Nigel Risner
Richard Wilkins

The Chartered Institute of Housing
Trish
Rob IT
Bernard, Dorothy, Jen and Colin
Jasper
Martyn DVD
The White Hart, Nigel, Woody, Owen, Jim, Stu, Scott, Andy, Odfellows, Debbie, Chloé, Matt, Sal, Bryn, Gabi and Richard
The Professional Speakers Association
Graham Beeley
Sue and Sara from Word4Word

Preface

Let me paint you a picture.

Imagine for a moment...

An organisation buzzing with highly motivated people...

People who actually love coming to work and are passionate about delighting customers...

People who are actively contributing to creating a vibrant culture and an incredibly successful business.

An organisation that is recognised as the best by customers and competitors...

Is this just an impossible dream?

No...

The most successful organisations understand the importance of putting people first. They believe that it works. And because they *believe*, it does.

They are winners and their results speak for themselves.

Come with me on a journey that will lead you to inspire your people and create a truly brilliant business.

CHAPTER 1

Customer Care is Dead!

*To create a successful business
and positive culture, you need to go to
the very soul of an organisation.*

People often say to me:

'Liam, can you help us improve customer services at our organisation? This month we need to "do" customer care. Let's tick all the boxes, print a service standard leaflet and a strategy and send it out to all our employees.'

And what happens to it?

When I'm giving a talk, with my handily placed rubbish bin on a table, this is the point at which people will shout out:

'It's filed!'

'It's put on a shelf!'

Until eventually somebody will call:

'It's chucked in the bin!'

Of course, they are all right. Absolutely nothing happens to it. Nobody bothers to read it – except possibly the policy officer. Have you ever known anybody who reads these things, or even remembers them?

No, neither have I.

You see, traditional customer care really is dead! It went out of fashion somewhere in the early 1980s. People *hate* customer care. They despise it with a passion.

How many people do *you* know who've attended a customer care training course? How many people do *you* know who enjoyed it? How many people do you know who've booked their holiday to coincide with a course? How many people do you know who've booked their sick leave to coincide with a customer care course?

Exactly! I rest my point.

If we are really going to deliver fantastic customer service and create a successful organisation, we need to go much deeper – right to the very soul of an organisation.

> ## "...we need to go much deeper – right to the very soul of an organisation."

We have to create a vibrant, energetic culture where people take a pride in their work and in their company:

- Where people, customers and colleagues come first. Every time

- Where people are inspired to be the best they can be. Every day

- Where people understand what they are contributing to and have fun at the same time

And let me tell you a little secret here... because I have good news for you.

Embracing cultural change at this deeper level is something not many companies bother with, but those that do are fantastically successful – Asda, Richer Sounds, WL Gore, to name but a few.

Many businesses carry out lots of customer satisfaction surveys – quite rightly, of course. Yours may even be one of them.

But what about your people? How do they feel about working for you? Are they proud of their company? Do they understand what they are there for? Do they really know why they come to work every morning?

"Do your people really know why they come to work every morning?"

An essential starting point for any cultural change or customer service programme is to do an employee morale survey. It doesn't have to be complicated. It needs just a few questions to establish the truth, and to find out what people feel and whether they are motivated to share your aims. Once you have the results of a survey like this, you have a clear benchmark to gauge your progress.

So you can forget all those boring customer care courses! If you can create a brilliant place to work, with a shared purpose and direction, you can achieve amazing things. Happy people = happy customers.

In fact, I'd like to make one simple but vital alteration to that last statement...

Happy, focused people = happy customers.

You need to have people in your business who understand what they are contributing to and why they are there. What is their purpose?

'No customers' means 'no business'. Simple really.

And here's the best news yet... What all this means is that you have the opportunity to achieve a competitive advantage over your opposition. It's up to you. If you *want* to do it and you are willing to relentlessly pursue your aims, you *will* realise your ambitions and you *will* deliver truly outstanding customer service.

My aim in this book is to give you some ideas to help you along the way.

I have also written this book in order to inspire you to achieve your ambitions at work *or possibly* in your personal life. My goal is that you will take something away with you that will make a difference – it doesn't matter how small or large, but there *will be* a difference.

> "My goal is that you will take something away with you that will make a difference – it doesn't matter how small or large, but there will be a difference."

Oh, and let's have some fun on the way!

I first became interested in culture change when I was working as an employee at a large housing association in Telford.

At a meeting to discuss some of the problems we had at the time with poor customer service, somebody suggested doing a customer care service standard leaflet.

Perhaps you've heard the same thing in your company:

'Come on, let's do customer care this week (month/year)!'

Well, I completely lost it. In the rant that followed, I declared to the meeting that leaflets and service standards would make no difference at all. Not to our people, to our services or to our company.

I went on to say that, if we really wanted to do something different, we would have to make radical, far-reaching changes that went to the very core of the business, to the culture. I know that sometimes you have to produce service standards and other things because public sector organisations are

closely monitored by the government. But in the end, it is passionate people who provide great services and not just words on a page.

Soon after my tirade, I became the culture change manager for that company, and I still hold those strong beliefs today as a successful consultant and speaker.

What is culture you might ask? One of the best definitions I have ever heard is: 'It is just the way we do things around here.' It's the way you treat each other, your customers and competitors. It is the very essence and soul of your business.

"Culture is... the very essence and soul of your business."

Customer care is dead. Long live a service-excellence-focused culture that makes a *difference* to people's lives.

Don't feed the ducks...

- Inspire your people

- Carry out an employee morale survey

- Happy people = happy customers (or happy, focused people = happy customers)

- Shoot traditional customer care trainers!
  (Or at least, show them the door!)

- Create a positive 'can-do' culture

CHAPTER 2

Thanks for the Memories

*We all reach a tipping point
in business and our personal lives.
The moment when
something changes for good!*

You will sometimes reach a tipping point in your business. Perhaps you have right at this moment. It's a time when you just know that you have to change things. Whatever the reason – financial pressures, people pressures, boardroom pressures – you have reached that defining moment: the tipping point. The moment when you are going to take action to change things for good.

This book can help you make the change and, once the business starts to tip in the right direction, it will take on a positive momentum all of its own.

Perhaps there are a number of tipping points in your life or business. It took one of those moments for me to realise my true aim in life – to help change businesses and lives. I am now a successful author, consultant and motivational speaker. Some of my family wouldn't believe it. I sometimes don't believe it.

But my mom certainly would.

I can still see it vividly now, the milk bottle crashing down on my mom's head as my dad attacked her. His crazed, drugged eyes and the frenzy of the vicious assault.

It all seemed so mad, so brutal.

I didn't know what to do. I wanted to help my mom, to protect her, but it was all happening so fast. The screaming, the noise, mom was shouting 'Get out, go and get help!' I didn't want to leave her, it was unbearable, I couldn't go, but she shouted again for me to run. Tears streaming down my face, I fled to the next door neighbours for help.

I was six years old. At first it had seemed like a normal night. And then he just flipped. My mom was just over five feet tall and the most incredibly caring person you could ever meet. My father's other, darker personality had taken over. I had seen it happen many times before. After that night, I only saw him rarely – usually in a mental health hospital or some sort of 'care in the community' place.

Many years later, I was to see him one final time as I identified his body following his suicide.

The experience of that night of violence was to shape the rest of my life. Of course, I didn't realise it at the time and it was not until 36 years later that I realised how much it had made me the person I had become.

I now realise that in a strange way it had an incredibly positive effect on my life. Sometimes it is about making good out of bad – something I am still trying to do.

So what is your first childhood memory?

Has anybody ever asked you that question?

I was attending a meeting of the Professional Speakers Association in Birmingham and was sitting next to a really friendly person called Don. Suddenly, the speaker said 'Everybody has a story to tell, all of you have been through some amazing things in your life. I want you to turn to the person next to you and tell them your first memory as a child.'

In an instant, I remembered the night that had been hidden deep in my mind. It was something that I had obviously wanted to bury and forget. But that question had acted as a trigger to my forgotten thoughts. I knew immediately that there was no way I could tell the truth. I just couldn't talk about it and then be asked to explain it in front of the crowd. I made something up about being asked to sing at a birthday party, but my head was spinning. I was no longer in the room.

That night really made me question what I was doing with my life and what I wanted to achieve.

Let me explain a little bit more.

My mom divorced my father and for many years brought me up as a single parent. We were moved from family to friends until finally we got a council house in Shifnal, Shropshire. I can still remember the look on my mom's face and her pride when she finally held the keys in her hands. People often scorn others as being different, or even inferior, if they are brought up on a council estate. That is rubbish. I'm no different to anyone else. I am a council house kid and proud of it! It didn't stop me achieving my aims.

My mom was a fantastic person and an inspiration. She would do anything for me and brought me up always to be positive. She would never say anything discouraging – it would always be 'You can do it, go on, have a go at it!' Instead of 'Don't have stupid dreams', it would be 'Make your dreams come true!'

I was always made to believe in myself and feel that anything was possible. Other people are not as fortunate as me and don't have that person who motivates them to make something of their life.

From that terrible night when I was six years old, my mom dedicated her life to me and turned a nightmare into a positive event that has shaped my life for the better. I was emotionally scarred by this incident, along with other events, and for my early years at school I was always in the slow class. I realise now how I have been affected by those early memories all my life. I couldn't read or write until long after my friends had learnt. I lacked self-confidence and was insecure. My mom gave me the platform to build a great life.

She was an incredible motivator and could connect emotionally with people from all backgrounds. Other people in my family thought that I might be a lost cause because of my early disturbed childhood, but my mom gave me love, attention and the confidence to keep doing things differently and believing in myself.

That night in Birmingham, my childhood memory gave me a sudden insight into who and what had inspired me to be the person I am today. I realised that my mom was the reason that I have done some successful things in my life and have never been scared of doing something differently or taking on a challenge.

I had reached a tipping point, the moment where I had a clear realisation of what I wanted to do with my life.

My mom was a really passionate person. If I can take just a little bit of her passion, energy and inspiration into my life I will be happy. My aim is to inspire others to change their businesses or to make their own or their loved ones' lives better. In this difficult world, whether it is about changing our business or our personal life, we all need hope, confidence and belief that we can indeed make our dreams come true.

Belief is the key.

"If you believe in something enough and are determined to make it happen, more often than not it will come true."

Perhaps, just as importantly, if you can persuade other people to believe in you or your business aims you will be amazed at the results. The people in your business are your X factor – your excellence factor, if you like. If you harness their energy and commitment, you will be amazed at what you can achieve.

This stuff is really powerful, and the great thing is that you will be creating a competitive edge because not many people do it. They totally underestimate the potential of their people. In fact sometimes, amazingly, they see them as a major problem! One chief executive, who will remain nameless, once said to me, 'I know that this might sound negative, but I have 167 threats working for me.' You're damn right it's negative! Turn it around! You have 167 people working for you and 167 opportunities to help you achieve the most incredible things. It is just a mindset really, a mindset that needs changing.

What sort of business do you want to create? What do you want to achieve?

Have you reached the tipping point in your business? Sometimes the important thing is just to understand that you have reached that defining moment and that you need to take action to make a change. Go on... tip the balance in your favour!

> "...you need to take action
> to make a change.
> Go on...
> tip the balance in your favour! "

Don't feed the ducks...

- Turn negatives into positives

- Dare to dream

- Believe in yourself and your ideas

CHAPTER 3

Smell the Culture, Shock the System

To begin cultural change
within a business, you must create
a sense of urgency.

Many people ask me questions such as the following:

- 'How can I create a successful culture at my organisation?'

- 'How can I continually delight customers?'

- 'How can I create a top performing company?'

There are no simple answers, of course. Just a number of key steps that need to be taken on the path to creating a place where people are really proud to work. (The cultural change table at the back of this book will help you understand the key steps in the change process.)

Whether yours is an underachieving organisation struggling to provide great customer service, or a good organisation perhaps a little complacent with the way things are going, the only way to start a major culture change programme is to shock the system and create a sense of urgency.

When you go into a restaurant, a shop or a business for the first time, do you immediately get a feeling about the sort of service you are going to receive? Is there something about the decoration, the temperature, the branding, the general feel you get about the place, or perhaps the look of cold aggression on the receptionist's face?

Think about this for a minute. How long does it take you to understand how well you are going to be treated?

Granted, I do this for a living. But when I walk into an organisation, I can almost smell the culture and sometimes it doesn't smell very good at all. In fact, sometimes it reeks of demotivated people who couldn't care a monkey's uncle about providing any type of customer service.

I often use this sign in my speeches to illustrate the point:

We can only please one person per day.
Today is not your day.
And tomorrow does not look good either!

You know what I mean. You walk into a pub, for instance, and you wonder whether you have discovered some mysterious potion that makes you invisible. You are standing there patiently waiting to be served while the three people behind the bar are merrily chatting away to each other about who has won the latest reality TV show. They are completely oblivious to the fact that you are standing there holding a crisp £10 note and waiting for their lovingly tendered service. Then suddenly somebody walks in off the street and gets served straight away. Leaving you helpless and totally frustrated. Has it happened to you?

Yes, I thought so.

So what is going on? Why aren't the staff looking out for customers, aware of what is happening around them and displaying a sense of pride in the place they work and the service they provide?

They probably haven't been trained properly, which is the fault of the manager or owner (we will look at leadership later). Or perhaps they are the wrong people with the wrong attitudes. Again, this is something we will look at later in the chapter 'Hoovers Really Suck'. But whatever the reason, the culture and service stink and the place needs a rocket up the proverbial.

People often cannot see that there is a problem at all, even if it is staring them in the face. Indignantly they proclaim 'Customer service? A problem? What problem?'

When I go into any business, the first thing I do is talk to people to find out what the culture is really like. Have you ever heard any of these comments before?(Please replace the word 'customer' with 'tenant', 'patient','client', 'student' or whatever is appropriate to your business.)

- Some of our people are frightened of customers.
  They just don't like customers.

- If it weren't for the customers, everything would be fine.

- They're a *!*X*!*ing nuisance coming in here!

- I don't appreciate my name being given to customers.

- Customers have always been classed as an inconvenience.

- That's the tenth person to ask me that today;
  I can't believe it, bloody wasting my time!

- You'll see what they're like, you'll see!

- The customer gets in the way of doing the work.

- Customers think that the louder and more aggressively
  they shout, the more they will get, so they become
  louder and so on. The polite people seem to be ignored.

- We have a 'can't-do' or 'won't-do' culture.

These statements have been taken from my experience of
working with companies. Each one of them has actually been
said to me at some time.

Those who made these statements were displaying symptoms of a sickness. I like to call it the 'Can't Be Bothered Syndrome'. Characteristics of the syndrome may include:

- A '9 to 5' attitude

- Passing the buck

- Culture of complacency

- Disrespect towards customers and colleagues

- Lack of business focus

- No real ambition, aims or values

- Negative culture

Do any of these seem familiar to you?

Have a think about the culture in your organisation.

Think about the way people talk to customers and the way they talk to each other. Be honest with yourself and think about the real situation.

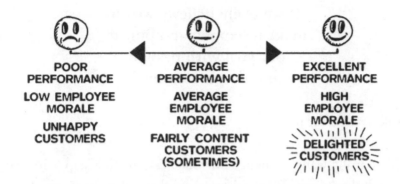

POOR PERFORMANCE	AVERAGE PERFORMANCE	EXCELLENT PERFORMANCE
LOW EMPLOYEE MORALE	AVERAGE EMPLOYEE MORALE	HIGH EMPLOYEE MORALE
UNHAPPY CUSTOMERS	FAIRLY CONTENT CUSTOMERS (SOMETIMES)	DELIGHTED CUSTOMERS

At one end of the scale, you have a rubbish place to work, demotivated employees and disgruntled customers. As you walk a little further along the line, you get a bit better, you become average and then good and then sometimes even very good. But right at the other end of the scale, you have a great place to work with highly motivated employees and delighted customers.

So how do we make that leap from good to great? What is the secret? There is a fantastic opportunity here because not many people understand how to do it.

So many people are stuck in the middle of this scale. Do you notice the connection between internal employee morale and service here? We have so many average businesses, councils, hospitals, housing and schools. Why can't we have truly brilliant businesses, councils, hospitals, housing and schools? The answer is: 'We can.' If we really believe, we can make it happen and pursue our goal with passion and determination.

> "If we really believe, we can
> make it happen and pursue
> our goal with passion
> and determination."

Ok, let's go for it!

If we really want to change our business, the first step is to shock the system. We need to create that sense of urgency I talked about earlier.

There is something about the culture of any organisation that is hard to define. People often say 'It's the way we do things around here.'

Our customers are no different. They know immediately what service they are going to receive. They, too, can smell the culture.

To break this negative culture, you have to draw a line under the past and start again. To create this sense of urgency, you need to give people a compelling reason to change for the better and begin to create a great place to work.

This might be something as serious as a company reorganisation that could mean redundancies. It could be a move to new offices, a merger, a government initiative, a cash crisis or other business pressures. Whatever it is, you need to create a sense of urgency – the need to do things differently to achieve better results.

If you aren't currently facing a situation like this that gives this sense of urgency, then create one now. Invent one if you have to but make sure you give people a real reason to change.

> "… you need to create
> a sense of urgency –
> the need to do things differently
> to achieve better results."

When you have decided on your reason to change, ensure you shout it loud from the rooftops. If this means holding a special management meeting, creating a one-off newsletter or just generally telling everybody you know, that's fine. But leave people in no doubt about the seriousness of the situation. For instance:

If we don't change now, we will go out of business!

It may be as simple and straightforward as that. From reading this book, you will probably understand how much I believe in having superb internal communications people or systems. They can make or break your drive to create a cultural change.

You will need to leave a short period for the message to sink in. Then you will have to give people a new positive focus for the future. But let's save that for another chapter. For now...

Don't feed the ducks...

- Create a sense of urgency

- Communicate it strongly internally

- Leave no doubt about the seriousness of the situation

CHAPTER 4

Second from Bottom: Have You Got the Message Yet?

Create a strong internal and compelling vision for change – something that people can believe in!

Are you sitting comfortably, happy in the knowledge that to change a culture you need to create a crisis?

Good!

The only challenge we now have is to create a positive vision for the future, a vision that people want to be part of and believe in.

An organisation invited me in to do a bit of cultural 'guruing'. It was among 12 rivals that were delivering services to the same client. The client used the customer service league table to rank the rivals' performance – and this organisation was second from bottom.

I spent some time talking to people about the issues and quickly got a picture of the challenges they faced. Their internal communication systems were non-existent. It soon became clear that none of the employees knew they were second from bottom or that, if they didn't change things, they were likely to lose their annual multi-million pound contract.

I decided to make an emotional connection with all the employees. After I'd given them a number of urgencycreating briefings, we issued lots of posters showing the organisation second from bottom of the customer service league. Across the table, we stamped HISTORY in great big red letters.

The message was clear. You don't deserve to be second from bottom. You have good people, you are all working hard. If we all focus and pull in the same direction, we will move up that league.

> **"If we all focus and pull in the same direction, we will move up that league."**

It had an incredible effect on people. The phone lines started buzzing and over the next few weeks and months people were constantly asking 'Where are we in the table?' On top of this, we gave them a new positive focus of 'Getting customers connected' (to a telephone line).

Again the message was simple. Each employee was asked to imagine their own mother or other family member or perhaps a friend needing to be on line as quickly as possible. No matter whether they were in the front line or working behind the scenes, every person in that company could have a massive influence on getting people connected quickly. They could all make the difference. If they really wanted to, they would succeed in climbing that league.

The results were amazing: within three months, the organisation had moved from eleventh (second bottom) to fifth. They couldn't believe it, but it was really quite straightforward. We created a sense of urgency and then gave people a reason to change and something to believe in. The organisation had achieved their twelve-month target in less than three months. I strongly believe that the sharing of the league table, and the desire of employees to make it history, played a massive part in the success story. They had been emotionally hurt by the table and were motivated to do something about it.

> "We created a sense of urgency and then gave people a reason to change and something to believe in."

Whatever your focus or vision, it is vital to make it stick. It is no good creating something that people want to be part of and then just leaving it in a strategy document in a filing cabinet.

I once helped create a vision for a large company with over 400 employees and a multi-million pound turnover.

In this instance, the company had just gone through a large reorganisation and a number of people had been made redundant. It was important to bring some ambition back to the employees and lift them from the negativity and despondency that was engulfing them.

> "It was important to bring some ambition back to the employees and lift them from the negativity and despondency that was engulfing them."

The vision we decided to use was 'Creating a world-class company'. This caused some controversy with people saying we were aiming too high.

'You're joking,' they said, 'we can never achieve anything like "world-class" here.'

This is a typical reaction from people who have no ambition, or vision. So what should the aim be? To create a 'quite good company'! Ridiculous of course! You have to aim to be the best. You need to have the desire to reach for the stars or you will just end up being permanently stuck in the mud.

We backed the statement up with the following descriptions of the company:

- The best at what we do

- Recognised as the best by our customers and competitors

- A company where people are proud to work

Three simple, straightforward statements that people could understand and believe in. Even if they just remembered one part of it, at least they knew why they were turning up to work every day and what they were contributing to.

The ambition – the vision – was established, and I am delighted to say that this organisation is now starting to become a leader in its field and its reputation continues to grow. I am proud to have been involved in starting the process of building a world-class company.

To make the message stick, we put everybody through a day's training experience or re-induction to the company's new values. We spent this day explaining what these new values meant and how everyone could become involved in making the vision come to life.

Note: I always take this approach to any consultancy projects that I carry out. It is vital to inspire and involve people throughout any change project. People often make the mistake of getting the board to decide the vision and values of an organisation and take no notice whatsoever of the views of their employees. In fact they often ignore them.

After many board away-days, the employees in the company are frequently presented with something like the following:

OUR MISSION

We are here to serve communities and keep people safe in their homes, at the same time maximising the opportunities for community cohesion and development. We respect people and want to give all customers a better quality of life, improving the standard of properties as well as providing homes, not just bricks and mortar, for the future and affordable places to live. Customers come first.

(And if you can remember this in one minute's time you have won a prize!)

I am out of breath just reading all of that. How on earth is anybody going to remember the vision or be moved to take positive action?

All good, earnest, heartfelt stuff but can you honestly tell me that people are going to live these values every day at work. No chance! And what makes it worse is they have had no input in creating it at all. No input = no commitment. It might as well be written on toilet paper for all the lasting good it will do.

It is absolutely vital to involve people throughout the process and create a compelling vision that people really believe in. Something simple like:

People First
Putting customers and colleagues first
and making a difference
to people's lives.

This was a statement that I recently helped create with a large housing association. It's simple, emotive and, yes, the association's *people* were fully involved in the process.

Going back to my previous example, we also linked the values to the employee evaluation/personal development scheme. The question 'What have you done this year towards creating a world-class company?' was a new and vital addition to the evaluation form.

The chief executive took new employees, on their first day, through *Creating a World-Class Company*, an induction

booklet that explained what was expected of them. The
booklet also contained the following:

> *'If you don't think this is the company for you*
> *or that the values do not meet your own,*
> *think carefully if this is the right place for you*
> *to work. I would be happy to discuss it with you.'*

This was straight talking; it was vital to begin to create a
positive environment with passionate people with real
ambition. Not just for new starters but also for some of the
people who had been there for years. We were serious about
change and people had to understand that. It wasn't just
another 'flavour of the month'. This was just one of a number
of initiatives to ensure the vision was real and here to stay!

> "It was vital to begin to create a positive
> environment with passionate people with
> real ambition."

'Creating a world-class company.' These were not just words
on a piece of paper. They were the vital spark that inspired
people to believe they really could create something special at
work.

I am delighted to say they are still reaching for the stars
today!

Don't feed the ducks...

- Make an emotional connection

- Create a compelling vision

- Deeply embed the vision in the culture of the organisation

- Be ambitious. Don't be put off by the 'can't-do' brigade

- Be serious. It is your organisation, it is your life

CHAPTER 5

Can't be Arsed Ltd

*Surround yourself
with positive people and
deal with the time wasters.*

Before you start reading this chapter, I need to issue the following health warning.

If you suffer from a sensitive disposition and are easily offended by the harsh truth, please stop reading now.

Most of the people working for your organisation are hard-working and just want to do a fair day's work for a fair wage. Given the right motivation, direction and reward, they will deliver fantastic customer service and represent your business with pride. However, there are a few people, who I like to call negative leaders, who take great pleasure in destroying your business on a daily basis.

Sometimes somebody will come up to me after I've given a speech on positivity and say 'Liam, that's all very well but I've been working here for 25 years and this is a crap company to work for!'

Now, utterly amazed by this remark, I could say 'What are you constructively doing to change things for the better?' Or, and possibly the best option, 'If you have worked here for 25 years and things are that bad, why don't you go and work somewhere else where you can be happy? Why not go somewhere far away from here, where your depressing attitude will not have a negative effect on your colleagues and the success of this business?'

You see, we are not very good at dealing with these types of people. With all our politically correct, draconian employment laws, we are frightened to say 'Thanks very much but here's your P45. Go and demotivate some other poor unfortunate souls!'

Now be honest here. You must know the type. How about the person who has been working on reception for 15 years and has a terrible attitude to you and your customers? Let's call this person Gerry the Gatekeeper. The problem is all the gates are locked and Gerry has the only key. Everybody knows about Gerry – his scowl is legendary. Gerry is truly the most difficult and sometimes downright rude person you have ever met.

Well, if you have a Gerry, why on earth is he still working there? Why are you allowing him to stay? So that he can systematically, on a daily basis, set about killing your business?

"Gerry kills your business stone dead!"

I know it isn't easy, but people like Gerry need to be challenged, not accepted. If you can't inspire them to change, then fire them. You will not only be doing your customers a favour but also your long-suffering colleagues who are continually ground down by their attitude and behaviour.

Ask yourself this question. If this was your business, would you put up with somebody who regularly damages your reputation and has the potential to be the reason you go bust? The thing is, though, it is your business! Whether you own it or not, it is yours! You are passionate about it, you want it to succeed! Don't put up with these people. If they can't make the effort, tell them to go and work for Can't Be Arsed Ltd up the road.

I once sat in a meeting where a chief executive was addressing around 30 people on the very serious issue of restructuring the organisation and the fact that there might be job losses. Just next to me, somebody started snoring, gently at first and then louder and louder. Despite the best efforts of his neighbour to nudge him awake, the guy kept falling asleep again. Needless to say, he quickly became one of the casualties of the reorganisation.

The crucial thing is that you identify these people and, when the opportunity arises, move them on. As the saying goes, get the right people on the bus (business) in the right seats (jobs) and drive it in the right direction. Then get the wrong people off the bus as soon as possible. (See Good to Great by Jim Collins.)

Another chief executive I know asked all his senior managers to identify their stars – the people who should be looked after at all costs. He also asked them to identify the people who were making no contribution to the business whatsoever. He kept that list with him and regularly asked the managers what they were doing to improve the situation. In my travels around various companies, I have come across many inspiring people. I have also come across a few characters who have a total disrespect for their customers, colleagues and the company they work for. I don't have the time of day for them. They love you to fail, they delight in your struggles, they celebrate failure. Don't let them destroy your business. Do something about it now!

In one final tale on this subject, I once knew somebody who was the office postman at an organisation I worked for. He happily went around delivering his post to the relevant departments and telling everybody who listened that it was a rubbish company to work for and he was going to go and live and work in Spain. Eventually he achieved his dream and went to live in Spain. Six months later, when things didn't work out, he was back working for the same company delivering the post and moaning on about what a rubbish company it was to work for. Some people just can't see it, can they?

And with that message, I rest my case m'lud!

Don't feed the ducks...

- Inspire or fire

- Challenge negative attitudes

- Get the right people on the bus (business)

- Get the wrong people off the bus

- Drive it in the right direction

CHAPTER 6

**it Happens!

Passionate leadership and strong values are essential to create a positive culture and successful business.

'Let's talk about **it!'

These were the rather direct words that David Birkett greeted me with as I walked into his office.

David is Managing Director of Serious, an organisation committed to dealing with waste disposal and improving the environment.

He is passionate about people and passionate about his company. His passion has led him from starting a business from scratch from his front room to achieving a near £3 million annual turnover. David expects to double that over the next few years.

What was the catalyst in his success? He started receiving a number of calls from clients complaining about things his employees were doing. He couldn't understand what was happening because his people and vehicles were nowhere near the places mentioned at the time.

It transpired that a competitor had started to imitate the livery of his company and their fleet of vehicles was being mistaken for his.

He knew there was only one thing to do and that was to completely rebrand. However, he didn't want to do a run-of-the-mill job. David decided to take the opportunity to instil a new set of values at the same time.

OUR VALUES

OPEN
Openness means we're up front about
what we do and how we do it.
We design, install and maintain
sewage and waste water systems –
nothing more, nothing less.

A SENSE OF HUMOUR
We're called Serious, but we treat
what we do with a touch of wit.
Our whole brand
reflects our sense of humour.

STRAIGHT TALKING
We tell it straight –
no jargon, gobbledegook or spin.
The last thing our customers want
is a load of waffle.
We get to the point.

RESPONSIBLE
We say what we do and we do what we say.
When we are given a problem to solve,
we deliver without fail. Our customers
must be confident that once something has
been entrusted to us it'll be taken care of.

He employed a top marketing company who had a history of success in dealing with blue-chip companies.

'It cost me an arm and a leg but it was worth every penny. Since rebranding, turnover has gone up nearly 75%. They had to convince me that it would work and they did.'

David is serious about the environment and his business, and Serious is the new name of his company: try logging on to www.weareSerious.co.uk to see for yourself. Although it is a serious business, fun is a central theme of his business. Anybody with a mission statement of '**it happens' has just got to have a sense of humour.

David also told me about another big change that happened after the new values were introduced, something that I have seen happen often during a period of culture change.

'We have some great people here now, but some of the people just couldn't handle the change. They were so negative about it that they were almost like internal terrorists. Complaining about things all the time, upsetting others and just generally resisting the change. They were dedicated to seeing us fail.

*'The new values and rebranding saw a
25% turnover in staff. This was a good thing.
If the staff didn't believe in what we were doing,
it was time for them to go. The amazing thing
was that they decided to go themselves.
One by one, they made their mind up that
this vibrant, new positive culture wasn't for them.
We have never looked back since!'*

David Birkett has created a place where people really want to come to work. He has inspired his team to be as enthusiastic about their work as he is and, at the same time, think about the positive impact they are having on the environment.

*'At a recent team meeting, my managers
came up with a new statement that
sums up what we do really well:
"Save the world from waste by helping others."
Everybody here knows what they are doing,
why they are doing it and what they are
contributing to.'*

David understands the importance of delivering exceptional customer service. All his men are given branded overalls: 'They look good, they feel good, so they deliver better service.

There are a lot of cowboys in this industry. I like to get the job done right.'

There are some fantastic lessons to be learned from David. He had the vision to employ a top company to carry out his branding. It initially cost him a lot of money but he was looking towards the long-term profitability of the company.

This innovative approach has made his business really stand out from the competition. Not only has he massively increased his turnover, his reputation has also grown with national media coverage of his new brand.

David has also instilled new values as a foundation to the brand. Some people left and fought hard against the change but he is now reaping the rewards of his brave decision to do something different in an industry that is not noted for its innovation.

It was a pleasure to meet David. Every time I meet somebody like him it convinces me more that you have to be passionate about your business if you are going to succeed.

And if you can be passionate about **it, you can be passionate about anything!

> "You have to be passionate about your business if you are going to succeed."

Don't feed the ducks...

- Be innovative with your branding and stand out from the crowd

- Develop meaningful values that people believe in

- Be passionate about your business

- Persuade the internal terrorists to leave as soon as possible – they are killing your business

CHAPTER 7

Keep the Dream Alive

Create a team of positive ambassadors to ensure lasting cultural change.

I hope you now have a clear idea of how you can change your culture in order to start seeing delighted customers flocking through your doors. I hope you are also feeling motivated to get out there and change your business, your department... or even your life.

In many ways, the start of the change process is the easy bit. it is making your culture stick that can be the really challenging part.

When I start a culture change project I like to carry out a cultural Audit of what makes the business tick, by talking to as many people as possible. I like to call it the O'Connell Way. This ensures that I look at the big picture: not only the instant 'shock the culture' start but how, once you've got the scrum moving, you can keep the momentum driving forwards – year after year.

I have already mentioned a number of elements that are vital to help create a vibrant culture. These include:

- Shocking the culture and creating urgency

- Creating a compelling vision

- Having values that are universally shared

Now is the time to consider creating a team of cultural architects to ensure the positive culture you are building has solid foundations. It is important that, once you have created a culture that people believe in, they continue to make it come to life in the workplace.

When I am asked to help improve a company's customer service or culture, I initially carry out a number of training experiences to help move the organisation forwards. However, the messages don't just stop the minute the people walk out of the training room. How many training courses have you been on where you've felt you've got something out of it but then, as soon as it's finished or a few weeks later, you have forgotten all about it? What is the point? What a waste of money! During my training experiences, I ask people to really be honest and open and come up with a number of ideas to help them improve their organisation. Everybody has something to contribute towards moving their organisation forwards.

When working with me in these sessions, people can talk about the issues, of course. But what I really want are positive actions, vibrant ideas to help change the culture. These are not just the ideas of management, or the board of directors, they are everybody's ideas. After all, it is everybody's company and, if things are going to change, everybody has to be included.

I often say to people 'This is your company, nobody else's. It is not up to somebody else to change things. It is up to you. Start now by doing something, just one thing, a little bit differently.'

Some of the discussion prompters I might use are:

- What would make you proud to work for your organisation?

- What are your customers' perceptions of your organisation?

- How can you alter those perceptions?

- Put yourself in your customers' shoes. What is it like and how can you improve things?

Following the sessions, I create a report of actions to help the organisation continue the momentum for change. This ensures that the messages and ideas of all the employees are properly captured and represented. How many times do you hear employees say 'We know what the problem is, but management never listen'? Frontline people really are the experts. They know what is going on; all you have to do is ask them.

I then recommend that the 'guiding team', 'cultural architect' or 'champion group' is created. Call them what you like, the idea is to create a group of active, enthusiastic, passionate people. I also strongly recommend that an overall 'customer champion' role is created. This is essential to ensure the process is driven internally. Although it can be seen as expensive, it is probably one of the most cost-effective things that any business can do. The investment will pay for itself many times over but it is vital that the right person is appointed. I have had the pleasure to work with some great people in the champion position, all different in character but all with a huge desire and passion to achieve success for their company. It goes without saying that the management team has to be passionate and actively drive the change as well. If it isn't, ensure that you do something about it as soon as you can.

> "I ... strongly recommend that an overall 'customer champion' role is created."

Occasionally, at this point, I will come across some barriers that need breaking down. Frequently these form a part of the culture that needs changing in the first place. For example, most organisations want to see great customer service and create cultural change but they are not so happy to spend money to achieve it. Often the businesses I am working with have a turnover of multi-millions. It is a drop in the ocean to appoint a customer champion to drive the project when I am gone, but still people take some persuading to do it. So if you really want to make lasting change it is absolutely essential to spend the money.

When I'm working with a company, I would continue to act as mentor to the new customer champion to ensure that they have the knowledge and understanding to make a lasting mark. I would keep in contact to make sure things are on track, but at some stage the change process has to be undertaken from the inside. It is down to the champion and the champion group to lead the change process and encourage all employees to really embrace it.

This team will take ownership of the O'Connell Way action plan. We often call it something else, such as the People First Programme (something that reflects the drive and aim of the organisation), and ensure that all the suggestions are implemented. It is really important here that the internal communications systems are sound and that when any positive actions that employees have suggested are put into operation everybody is told about them. A word of advice here – never ever miss any opportunity to communicate a positive message to help your cultural change keep rolling forwards. Your passionate people need to be motivated.

"…never ever miss any opportunity to communicate a positive message to help your cultural change keep rolling forwards."

The other side of this coin is that your negative people hate success. They really despise it. If you keep communicating positive messages, you might find that some of your more destructive colleagues decide to leave. If you are lucky, this is often the outcome of a successful cultural change programme. Your team should be made up from all areas of the business, both senior and junior employees. This is vital to ensure that every part of your business is touched by a positive cultural ambassador. You will find that they continue to come up with many new ideas to bring about positive change. These teams tend to take on a life of their own. You will be amazed how enthusiastic people become when they can see their direct impact on improving the culture of their company.

The team itself must be empowered, made to feel special and given quality time to meet and implement the many actions that will be created. The ambassadors must be your most enthusiastic people. Your customer or cultural champion must have the respect of all your employees, or at least be well on the way to achieving that respect.

You already know who these people are. Inspire them and give them this opportunity. You will never look back!

plement the O'Connell

and give them quality time

ive people squirm and start to apply for

CHAPTER 8

Good Cop, Bad Cop

*Motivation and reward
are powerful when combined with
meeting difficult issues head on.*

Let's make one thing clear here. Cultural change is not just about the 'fluffy stuff'. It is linked to the cold reality of the situation – 'no customers' means 'no business'.

Some people may think that the motivational activity that I have talked about in this book is just superficial and that it can't possibly have a lasting effect on an organisation. The good news is that it can and it does!

The organisations that persistently work at motivating their people with a shared sense of belief and direction are the top performers; they are the best at what they do.

This, however, is only one important part of the cultural change journey: there needs to a tougher element to the process as well.

When working on a brilliant change project at the University of Essex, I came across something that I like to call the 'good cop, bad cop' experience.

Actually it was Linda McCanna, a manager at the University of Essex, who gave me the title for this chapter. Many thanks Linda – the drinks are on me!

Linda is the bad cop in the scenario. Without going into too many details about their particular project, Linda manages about 140 people who deal with the accommodation services for the university students.

The challenge that we faced was moving the organisation from a good (in fact very good) business to a great business.

As I normally do, I recommended that they appoint a customer champion to drive the change project internally. A brilliant enthusiastic person called Darren Baker took on this responsibility. Darren is the good cop.

You will already know that I base any change project on the principles of:

Happy, focused people = happy customers

This is about attitude, strong direction and other motivational factors – all the things that I discuss at length in future chapters.

Linda, our bad cop, faced a challenging attendance/ sickness record with a number of people taking a totally unsatisfactory number of days off work. This was affecting morale and the ability to deliver services. It had almost become an accepted part of the culture.

Linda tackled the problem head on and introduced a tougher, more rigorous attendance management system.

As with any change of this nature, this development was initially unpopular and the union and some staff had reservations.

It was an incredible success! In the first month that the system was introduced, sickness was cut by 19%. In the second month, it had an amazing 52% success. Over 50% fewer people were off in May compared with the same month the previous year.

Linda had tackled the issue. It had been unpopular but it worked. People were delighted. There were more people in work and that meant there was less pressure on individuals. Uncomfortable change had brought brilliant results. Linda's new, tougher system had been a great achievement.
(Important note: Linda McCanna is not just a bad cop. She is a highly motivated and successful manager who really believes in the importance of motivating people.)

At the same time as this bad cop activity was taking place, our good cop, Darren in his champion role, was working with me and the senior management team to create a brilliant place to work, a values-driven momentum and a feel-good factor.

To thank employees for winning an award for customer/
student excellence, the university held a prize draw with a top
prize of a weekend in London for two with tickets for a top
West End show. They were motivating their people in many
different ways. To name just a couple of things, they were
taking managers out for lunch to engage them in the cultural
change process and to explain why it was happening, and
they were involving employees in creating new directions and
values for the organisation. There were many initiatives
planned, including a fantastic launch event and the creation
of an innovative employee reward and customer service
programme called 'Magic Moments'.

Darren was a very good 'good cop'. He understood the
importance of reward and motivation. But most of all, the
whole senior management team recognised the importance of
taking a balanced approach to the change process.

BAD COP

**Deal with the tough stuff,
disciplinary issues, attendance records,
performance, attitude and behaviour.**

GOOD COP

**At the same time motivate,
inspire and reward people.**

The other vitally important issue is timing. If you have to tackle particularly challenging issues or behaviour, do it first! Create the tipping point, the sense of urgency, the storming phase and then (or at the same time) do the motivational stuff.

It really is bad cop first and then good cop. If you do a great launch event, develop new values and a shared direction that results in highly motivated people and then hit them with a new sickness system, a reorganisation or something equally challenging, it will not work. You might never be able to pick people up or motivate them again. Timing is everything. The cultural change programme is designed to give you the ability to challenge poor performance and attitudes.

Set the purpose. Agree the values. Measure performance and attitudes against these values. Use mystery shopping, customer attitude surveys – whatever it takes.

This is absolutely vital. I cannot emphasise enough how important this is. Create a great place to work, a vibrant atmosphere, but then ensure people deliver, perform, achieve. Any way that you want to put it really. At the end of the day, any business is based on the bottom line: results!

The senior management team at the University of Essex Residential Services are doing a great job. They have some brilliant people and will succeed in delivering an unforgettable experience for their customers.

I recently got a call from Darren and I was delighted when he told me;

> *"Accommodation Essex at the University of Essex has won the best accommodation in the UK, 2009. This is a customer service completed by students at over 80 universities.*
>
> *Over the last three years we have been working closely with Liam. His off the wall, invigorating and inspiring approach to cultural change has been hugely successful and this award is testament to the success of the cultural change programme.*
>
> *Our staff are delivering fantastic service to our customers and enjoying doing it. Now our people really are the difference and we could not have done it without Liam's help"*

Darren Baker
Business Development Manager
Accommodation Essex

Don't feed the ducks...

- Tackle difficult issues head on

- Get the balance right – good cop, bad cop

- Measure performance and attitudes

- Deal with poor attitudes

CHAPTER 9

The Duck Shoot

*To be successful in business or life,
you need to
keep trying different things,
innovate and stay one step ahead.*

So there I am hurtling through a wide open expanse of land with a rather startled cameraman and an eccentric member of the aristocracy at the wheel. Stunned, crazy-eyed deer are running wildly, scattered by the careering Land Rover and its violently throbbing engine.

As we hurtled along, I started to think that my favourite little plastic ducks have certainly led me to some very strange places.

It was meant to be a video shoot for my website. I would sit in a rowing boat with some of my plastic duck friends for company, very similar to the picture on the back cover of this book. Originally I had intended to do the shoot on a small boating pond but, due to insurance costs and various other frustrating problems, we couldn't get a suitable place.

The video company, Lightsource, came to the rescue. They knew a local landowner who owed them a favour. Before you know it, I am sitting in the middle of the most amazing mile-long lake and trying with all my might to stop myself drifting totally out of control. You really need to check out the video on my website to see the look of agony on my face.

I couldn't believe it. This was private land, in the owner's family for generations. It was never open to the public and it was beautiful. Simply stunning. I wouldn't have minded but the dustbin full of yellow plastic ducks looked slightly out of place in this beautiful countryside.

I just sat there amazed at how it had all happened.

The landowner wouldn't take no for an answer and insisted that he took us on an all-expenses-paid trip of his estate. Martin, my ever brilliant but slightly dazed cameraman, thought it was 'bloody amazing'. I don't think he could quite believe what was going on. 'Liam, these ducks certainly take you to some strange places,' he said.

When I first thought of the ducks a few years ago, I didn't have the faintest idea where it would lead me. But without ideas, without action, without doing something different to make things happen, nothing changes in your life or at work.

> "But without ideas, without action, without doing something different to make things happen, nothing changes in your life or at work."

Successful people and businesses never stand still. They are always trying to improve, always looking for the next step forward. They are always one step ahead of their competitors in planning the next phase of their life.

My life is constantly changing. I think I am just the sort of person who always sets challenges and wants to do something different. Because of my difficult early childhood, perhaps I am trying to prove something to myself. Perhaps I need the comfort of success and the acceptance of people generally. I'm not sure.

Have a look at my illustrated life story on page 180. I have done so many weird and wonderful things. Not all have worked but many have. It doesn't really matter if they occasionally fail – the main thing is to keep doing and trying different things. It helped me to look at my life as a series of cartoons, to understand the events that have made me the person I am now, both good and bad. Sometimes we need to make time and take a long hard look at our life or business to make sense of it all.

> "Sometimes we need to make time
> and take a long hard look at our life or
> business to make sense of it all."

I have come across a few very successful companies who have set aside creative time for their employees to devote to thinking differently, to help move the business forwards. Anybody can do it. If you don't innovate, you just stand still and, eventually, you'll start to go backwards.

> "If you don't innovate, you just stand
> still and, eventually, you'll start to go
> backwards."

The life story idea came to me as I was having a quiet pint in my local. My best ideas often come when I put quality time aside to think in a relaxed atmosphere. It is just the same in business; we need to create time for people to think – not just about 'business as usual' but about 'business as unusual'. We need to encourage different thoughts, perhaps even crazy ideas. Don't be scared to be different. Given enough time and commitment you could come across the one idea that will change your business for good.

"Don't be scared to be different."

As I mentioned earlier, my mum instilled in me a 'can do' attitude and one thing I'm certain about is that you have to do something to get something out of life. Sometimes you have to take a risk. Whether that be a breakneck ride in a Land Rover desperately clutching a bin full of ducks, starting a highly successful business or doing something new and exciting with your existing business or life, if you don't do, you don't get!

Don't feed the ducks...

- Do something different if you want a successful business

- Enjoy the strange things that happen: they may never happen again

- Never be scared to be different: you never know where it might take you

- Business as unusual, not just business as usual

- Devote some serious time for creative thinking:
if you don't have new ideas, you eventually go backwards

- Keep a tight hold of your ducks

CHAPTER 10

Inspirers, Dictators, Hippies and Chess Players!

Understand your leadership style and inspire your people.

As you set about your momentous challenge to create a customer-driven organisation, it is appropriate to sit down and assess your own leadership styles and how you are seen and judged by others. Strong, positive leadership is one of the biggest factors when creating a successful business culture.

This can be illustrated in a project in the north that I worked on a long time ago. It involved bringing together two very different cultures to form a new company. The potential for an almighty culture clash was huge. The whole tricky business needed to be handled sensitively or the new organisation could come down crashing and screaming.

Here is the scenario:

One organisation's leader is energetic, passionate and forward thinking, and realises that putting the customer first every time is not only important it is also essential if you are going to create a successful business. (By the way, as it happens, he does currently run a very successful business.)

John (I have changed his name here) recruits people in his own image. Because of this, his business is bursting with the energy and vitality of people who really focus on customers' needs.

I like to call this leadership style 'The Inspirer'. He positively leads his people towards a goal that is commonly shared by everyone in the organisation. He is sensitive to criticism but has created a fun, open culture and a great place to work.

I asked about 50 of his employees whether they had fun at work. The astonishing reply from virtually all of them was, quite simply, 'Every day!' In how many organisations will you find so many people who can say that? This is, I believe, their secret. They enjoy what they do. And they believe in it and therefore deliver unbelievable customer service.

The second leader is very different. I will refer to him as The Dictator.

He has a vision and he drives people relentlessly, almost coldly, towards it. He doesn't invite input from his people – he just focuses on achieving his vision. He has created a rather bureaucratic control- and system-led culture. His word is law.

He also runs a reasonably successful business. But, in my opinion, there could be much more focus on the importance of his people and the customer and potentially even greater success.

He also recruits in his own image. He has a team of solid, dependable and sound people around him. Do you see the potential for an almighty culture clash here? Of course you do.

It is important that these people are set free to bring about the change and realise the potential financial savings and improvements to services that the combination of both cultures can bring about.

But softly, softly though. Approach with caution. Don't scare or frighten The Dictator's organisation. Bring around change gradually. They won't be particularly used to innovation or thinking for themselves. In defence of The Dictator, though, The Inspirer's organisation can also benefit from some of the sound business practices that The Dictator can bring to the table. Remember that too much too soon can lead to the destruction of the entire business.

So are you an Inspirer or a Dictator? I know what my money is on, but you would know that by now having read this far.

Next from a different part of my work experiences comes The Chess Player – a chief executive I know very well, who is cool, calm and calculating. He always works three or four moves ahead. A brilliant strategist, he understands the importance of building a strong management team to carry out his plans. Not necessarily a great speaker, he relies on others with excellent people skills to do this for him.

He is ruthlessly determined to succeed and, make no bones about it, he does succeed. He is also very loyal to the people around him.

Finally we come to The Hippy. The Hippy leader just floats around, nothing seems to bother him, no crisis is bad enough to upset his dreamlike world. Hippy leaders often create a chaotic culture where people are frantically trying to achieve something, but there is no direction or focus.

Often the organisation only survives because of the quality of one or two members of the senior management team.

Hippy leaders are so laid back that, although often very likeable people, they are often a source of huge frustration to their employees. They also work on Hippy time: meetings start late and go on for hours, with seemingly little or no result.

A brief note on meetings. Please remember that there is only one thing worse in life than a business meeting and that is a follow-up meeting. If you have to hold a meeting, keep it short and to the point. Why waste three hours when an hour would be fine? I would hate to estimate how much productive time is lost each year to the wonderful phrase 'Let's hold a meeting to sort it out!'

So what are you: Inspirer, Dictator, Hippy or Chess Player? In all honesty, you will need a little of all of these qualities to build a successful organisation. You will certainly need a well-thought-out strategy and plan of attack. But from my experience, the really successful leaders are innovative passionate people, people who like people and who inspire them by their words and actions. If you are not naturally that sort of leader, employ somebody to help you who can do it for you. Cultural change nearly always starts from the top. Leaders put their stamp on things, positively or negatively, and people follow.

In this world, people are much more likely to want to help you if you treat them with respect and kindness. If you lead them on an optimistic journey with energy and imagination, you will succeed every time.

Don't feed the ducks...

- Inspire your people

- Create a fun and positive culture

- Keep meetings short and to the point

- Create a well-thought-out game plan

- Set your people free

- Hippy time is happy time but not at work!

CHAPTER 11

Inspire
Your People

*If you really believe in something
you can make
a difference to people's lives.*

Ron Dougan held the crowd in the palm of his hand. He was shaking as he spoke. As I looked out on the hundreds of faces in the audience, every one of them was transfixed by the man who at that moment was making a huge emotional connection with them.

Ron is Chief Executive of Trent & Dove Housing Ltd, which manages over 6,000 homes at affordable rents in the Burton upon Trent area.

Ron is passionate about his business and believes in creating homes and communities where people can live safely. I would like to share a little bit of his passion here with you now. Ron Dougan was brought up in inner-city Liverpool in the 1950s. He lived on the first floor of a three-storey house with his three brothers and sisters. His mum raised them after his dad went to sea and only managed to get home two or three times a year. They were a very close family. They had nothing really, but they were happy. The community was close and they didn't have a lot of money. Ron said 'There was no point in breaking into our houses because there was nothing there to steal anyway.'

Eventually, because of the overcrowding, they were moved to a flat in Croxteth, number 10 Curtana Crescent. It was great when they first moved in – the flat backed onto Lord Sefton's estate. The wildlife, the river and the open spaces made it a fantastic place for kids to play and live. 'You could wake up

in the morning and hear the birds singing.' Everybody got on
with each other and nobody caused any problems.

'Then suddenly our lives began to change.
The council altered their allocation policy and
started to move so-called "problem families" onto
the estate. Not just one family, but every week
a new family moved in. The council was using
the estate as a dumping ground. Dog muck
and worse still was pushed through our letterbox.
A general atmosphere of hate seemed to fill the
air. There was a quick turnover of people moving
in and out, there was no stability and that was
when the problems started to happen.'

Ron's mum had always brought them up to treat everybody
with respect – to understand the importance of good
manners and treating people properly. Some of the new
families didn't like this and had different values. Because of
Ron's family's behaviour, they thought they were different
from the rest and stood out from the crowd.

'We started to get bullied and picked on.
These were nasty people.
They just didn't care about anything or anyone.
It was a threatening and horrible atmosphere
and our lives were becoming a misery.

'One day, after many months of being bullied,
my brother and I were walking home and we were
set on again. This time we were beaten up badly.
'My mum was so angry and upset that she
immediately went around to confront the parents
who were responsible. Without any hesitation, the
mother dragged my mum out of our flat and beat
her in front of the neighbours and us kids.
My mum was never really the same again.
She was hurt and humiliated and developed
agoraphobia.

Our lives completely changed.
We were trapped in our own homes, helpless with
nowhere to turn. We went to the council for help
but they wouldn't do a thing; they would not lift
a finger to ease our pain.'

This was the story that Ron told his people at his employee annual conference that day. This was the reason, he told them, that he had got into the housing business in the first place. He wanted to create safe places to live, where people were not threatened and did not live in fear in their own houses. It was the driving force that had led him on his personal crusade to create safe communities.

The reason why Ron's audience of employees was so transfixed by the story was obvious. You could cut Ron's emotion with a knife. He was honest, he was real and he was making an emotional connection. I could see him shaking with feeling as he told the true story for the first time. The next day, the e-mails and messages of support started to flood in. It was becoming clear. People understood what they were all trying to achieve – it made sense why they came into work every day.

> "People understood what they were
> all trying to achieve – it made sense
> why they came into work every day."

Talk about motivating people and giving them direction! It was unbelievable, the positive effect it had on people. It would also have a massive effect on the customers of Trent & Dove Housing.

Some weeks later, as I walked around some of the new homes on the estates that Ron and his people were building, he said to me:

'Liam, I care and I make sure my people care. We are all committed here to trying to change people's lives. The area you are looking at used to be a notorious drug area with high crime and many social problems. We decided to knock it down and start again.

By working closely with the police, the council and voluntary services, we are making a huge difference to the quality of people's lives. I want to create homes where my sons Alex and Joe will feel happy to live. Fear is a terrible thing. If you have never experienced it, it is difficult to explain what it does to you. In the end, my mum finally managed to move us to a new place to live and our lives instantly changed for the better.'

Ron Dougan is a man driven by his own beliefs and experiences.

I have been lucky to work closely with Ron and his people to help him continue to create his dream. The work is not finished, it is an ongoing project, but I hope that, in some way, I have contributed indirectly to creating those communities that Ron so badly wants to see. It is about giving people a decent start in life, giving them the opportunity and sound base to build a life. Without a roof over our heads and a safe place to live, we have nothing.

Ron has created a brilliant place to work with committed people who understand what they are contributing to.

It was with real delight that I got a call from Ron to say that he had just won the National Housing Federation's Leader of Tomorrow award. Unsurprisingly, he had dedicated it to his own employees, who every working day are making a difference to people's lives.

Don't feed the ducks…

- Follow your passion

- Share your beliefs

- Inspire your people

- Change lives!

CHAPTER 12

Choose Your Attitude

*The importance of
choosing a positive attitude
to life and work.*

As I write this chapter, it is very early in the morning. Now I know this might seem strange but bear with me a minute. Most of this book has been written between the hours of 5 a.m and 8 a.m. in the morning.

I do this for a couple of reasons, one because I am at my most creative when I get up and two because it fits in with my lifestyle and allows me to do something else with the rest of my day.

However, it is not easy and it takes a hell of a lot of effort to actually drag myself out of bed to start work. Sometimes I really don't want to do it. But through my work over recent years, I have learnt something that has made a massive impact on my life... that you can choose your attitude. We spend so much time at work, why not enjoy it? Why not be passionate about it and consciously choose a positive attitude? As I type, it is dark outside and I can hear the wind and the rain rattling against the window. But I have made a choice. I want to be here writing these words. I want to try to create something interesting and special, something that might help give somebody some new ideas. I want to write a great book that helps my life keep moving forward. Simple as that. I have made the choice; I am here now in the moment.

In the film *The Dead Poets Society*, there is a line that sticks firmly in my memory. Seize the day! Make it extraordinary.

We have one life and one opportunity to live it. Make the most of it and choose a positive attitude.

"Seize the day! Make it extraordinary."

I first came across this choose-your-attitude method a few years ago when I read the book *Fish!* which is about a fish market in Seattle where the team of employees decided they wanted to create a great place to work. On a daily basis, they chose to enjoy themselves and have a good time, and, by the way, they sold fish. Loads and loads of fish, actually.

Imagine it: they start work really early in the morning, they are out in the open air and they are dealing with freezing cold, slimy fish day in, day out. But they made a choice to create a fantastic environment, with energy and passion, and become a world-famous organisation. They succeeded and the book became a best seller. They have made videos. People at my seminars tell me they have actually been to the Seattle fish market and it is brilliant – a real tourist attraction. They throw fish around and have fun with their customers. The people catch the energy, enjoy what they are doing and – of course – buy the fish.

It is a simple formula and underpins a lot of what I believe creates successful businesses. Great people, working in a fun environment where they are passionate about their work and about delivering fantastic customer service. And, as somebody at the fish market said, it has nothing to do with the fish whatsoever. The fish are just a by-product.

You have to find your own fish, your own way of having fun at work and creating a successful environment to work in. *Fish!* has been a massive influence on me, and I recommend that you read the original version.

> "You have to find your own fish,
> your own way of having fun at work…"

So to return to attitude – try it tomorrow or next time you go to work. What will you face? Meetings, loads of e-mails, customers. You have a choice. Are you going to have a good day or are you going to have a bad day? Are you going to have a good experience with a customer or a bad experience? It is up to you. You decide. In an instant, you can make the decision. Ask yourself the question: 'Good or bad?' Make the choice and choose the positive. You will be amazed what a difference it makes.

I was once speaking about attitude at a large conference in London. When I had finished, I saw this giant of a man coming towards me at speed from the back of the room. I was still checking my escape route when he said to me, 'Liam, I want to have a word with you about attitude. I recently went on a course of anger management sessions.'

I held my breath and began to dive for cover.
'Who makes you angry?' he bellowed, stopping me in my tracks.

Go on then, ask yourself the question: 'Who makes you angry?' Customers? Please, don't say customers! Family, friends, colleagues? Who makes you angry?

Without hesitation, the man from the anger management course said, 'You do! They told me that at the end of the day. It is *you* who makes *yourself* angry and it is *you* who can make the choice to keep calm and not lose your temper.'

> "It is **you** who makes **yourself** angry
> and it is **you** who can make the choice to
> keep calm and not lose your temper."

Try it with your family, your friends and your customers. It is simple. I guarantee it will make a massive difference to your life. You have to keep working on it, though, it doesn't come easy. Let me give you an example and perhaps you could decide whether I chose my attitude here.

It was eight o'clock at night and I was stationary on that not-so-wonderful car park otherwise known as the M6. It had been a really long day and I had been speaking somewhere down south. I was tired and all I wanted to do was get home to my wife Sue and take her out for a drink.

I was getting more and more frustrated but eventually I started moving and finally I arrived home.

But as I got in the door I noticed a letter on the table. Now I don't know about you, but I am one of those people who has to immediately open the letter. I can't just leave it. I have to have a look at it immediately.

So I opened it up and it was a letter from my bank. Already the stress levels are high and getting higher. Even worse, the letter said I was £367 overdrawn. Even worse than that, I had told them to transfer some money into that account a week ago to stop the problem happening in the first place. But help was on hand. There was the number at the bottom of the letter for 24-hour banking. I phoned the number and then went through one of the most frustrating customer service experiences you can ever have. We've all been there. Press 1 if you want to open a new account, 2 if you want a credit card, 3 if you want insurance, 4 if you are losing the will to live, 5 if you want to speak to a human being! Then suddenly I was lost in space and Dannii Minogue music came pumping out of the receiver. They couldn't even afford Kylie!

By this time I was really losing it and Jasper my golden retriever was taking cover under a table. Finally, and I still don't know how, I got through to somebody. Do you know what they said? 'You have got the wrong number'!

I couldn't believe it! I went mad and slammed the phone down. Then suddenly Sue said 'Stop! What are you doing?'

'You go around the country talking to people about choosing a positive attitude! What *on earth* are you doing?'

Sue was right. All I was doing was stressing myself out, and giving myself a potential heart attack. So I just stopped, put the letter to one side and phoned the right people calmly the next day. Who had caused all that problem? Me. Attitude is a choice, a state of mind. Choose the positive and save yourself a lot of heartache.

> "Attitude is a choice, a state of mind.
> Choose the positive and save yourself
> a lot of heartache."

Have you ever put petrol in a diesel car? I have and I confess to being a right plonker right here and now. I was with Sue at the time and had just driven out of the petrol station when the car started kangarooing down the road. After initially losing it for a few seconds and coming out with a few words somewhere along the lines of 'darn', 'blast' and 'oh dear' (thanks to my editor!), I decided to choose my attitude. We had a lot planned that day. What was the point in going mad and completely losing it? So I immediately phoned the garage and within an hour we were in a hire car carrying on with our day as planned. I had lost out in the pocket but I hadn't lost my temper. Believe me, this choose-your-attitude stuff really does work. Go on, try it for yourself!

If it makes sense to choose a positive attitude, what about choosing positive people to work with? But that's for another chapter! For now:

Don't feed the ducks...

• Choose a positive attitude

• Have fun at work

• Don't phone the bank when you are already stressed

CHAPTER 13

I'm Standing on the Edge of a Cliff in Cornwall

The customer always comes first,
wherever you might be.

What is great customer service? Obviously, being in the business and ranting on and on about service excellence, I have to ensure that I personally deliver a first-class service experience myself. This means taking and returning calls at any time or any place.

I was once on a much-needed break with a special friend. It had been a very busy time at work, with 16-hour days and thousands of miles of trailing up and down our glorious motorway network. I really needed to get away for a couple of days to recharge the batteries.

When we arrived at the suitably rugged Cornish harbour, we decided to go for a walk to freshen up. As I strolled along, I thought I should give my long-suffering wife, Sue, a ring to tell her we had arrived safely.

As soon as I turned the phone on, my answer machine and e-mail sprang into action. I had two messages from people who wanted to do work with me following a speech I had done in Blackpool. Now, here I was walking in the most fantastic place, with the sun shining and the wind blowing the cobwebs away and two business calls to deal with. What do I do? Ignore them until the following week or return them straight away? Although tempted to ignore them and continue our lovely stroll, I knew I had to phone them back immediately. You might think I should have kept walking. For some reasons, perhaps I should. And yet the call

I made led to me gaining a fascinating and *rewarding* contract.

Customer service is about being responsive to your clients. I got through to Mike Doran, a company director.

'Hi Mike, Liam O'Connell returning your call'.

'Oh, hi Liam, thanks for calling. Is it ok to talk? What are you doing at the moment, speaking at a conference or something?'

'No Mike, I'm standing on a cliff in Cornwall,' I responded.

'Don't do anything stupid. I know somebody from Samaritans who can help you!'

> ## "Customer service is about being responsive to your clients."

What followed was a really funny, quirky call that ended up with an invitation for me to go and speak to Mike about some potential business. I ended up doing some great work with him and his people, and his forward-thinking and successful organisation. Mike even gave me the title of the Can't be Arsed chapter you read earlier. Thanks Mike, by the way!

Once again I had made a great connection with my customer, a human connection, real and humorous. It was just about making the effort to call him, only a few minutes out of my walk and my life. Some people accuse me of being obsessed with my business. They might be right, but I would suggest that the most successful people and organisations do develop a positive obsession with their businesses and aims in life. A healthy obsession can bring positive results.

> "Develop a healthy obsession with your business!"

People really do appreciate a quick response. They remember it and it sets the tone for everything you do with them in the future. There is nothing worse than not returning a call. You hate it and your customers hate it. Make the effort, make the connection, make money!

Don't feed the ducks...

- Make every effort to return calls as soon as possible

- Put your customers first – always

- Don't jump off the cliff just yet

CHAPTER 14

The Luck of the Irish

*People make their own luck
by taking action.
Without action you achieve nothing.*

Has anybody ever said to you that you are a lucky person? That you are really lucky because you have a nice house, a good job and a lovely family? Or how lucky you are to run a hugely successful business with delighted customers, happy employees and huge profits?

Have you ever met anyone who's gone on and on about the fact that you are so lucky in life – your business is doing brilliantly, you travel the country meeting new people and you are doing what you enjoy? You really are a lucky, lucky person.

'I wish I could be so lucky,' they say mournfully.

This is total crap of course! You get out of life what you put into it. You get nothing without action.

Feeling sorry for yourself or talking about how unlucky you are to be running an average business achieves nothing. And yet, think for a minute, how many people do just that?

I once heard a story from a brilliant, passionate speaker called Richard Wilkins. I have taken the liberty of adapting it here.

Richard likes to refer to the 'sausage machine of life'.

Imagine a giant sausage machine. At one end you add the ingredients and at the other end, as if by magic, the finished sausage emerges.

Some people try to use the sausage machine of life but fail
miserably. They put a few ingredients in: perhaps a little bit
of negativity, and a pinch of can't-be-bothered here and a
scowl there. Then they go to the other end of the machine
and wait for the results. And they have a long wait. They say,
scratching their heads vigorously, why hasn't my life or
business changed? I can't understand it. So they go back to
the other end of the sausage machine and put the same
ingredients in again, negativity, can't-be-bothered, a scowl and
maybe a lack of self-confidence for good measure.

They then wait again for the results at the other end of the
sausage machine. And guess what! They are scratching their
heads in frustration because once again nothing changes in
their life. Opportunities don't seem to occur, people don't
want to help them. Where is that stroke of luck that will
transform their business? They keep on doing the same things
and waiting and waiting and waiting…

But just occasionally somebody will decide to change things
and put some different ingredients in the mix. How about a
little bit of positivity? A smile, a help-somebody-out here and
a smattering of take-a-chance there.

They walk to the other end of the sausage machine of life
and, lo and behold, things start to change! Doors start
opening for them and people start helping them to achieve
their aims. Their life and their business starts to change for
the better.

You see, the machine needs the right ingredients and the right approach, just like any successful business really; you only get out of it what you put in. Luck doesn't come in to it. If we act all miserable and grumpy and give out bad vibes, that is how people will react to us.

> *'Put the good stuff out there and you'll get the good stuff back. Give out better and you will become better. The world is a reflection of yourself.'*

Attributed to James Gormley, aged 19,
on the wall of the Studio, Cannon Street, Birmingham.

What is your aim in life? Perhaps it is to create a successful business, lose weight, stop drinking or get out of debt. (By the way, I have considerable experience of all of these and if you would like to share a pint with me I would be happy to expand on this.) Whatever your aim is, it is important to make up your mind that *you are going to do something about it.*

From today, I ask you to take a positive attitude to the challenges that confront you in life.

From today, commit to making the change and pursue it with focus and determination.

It is up to you; you have to want to do it. You have to believe that you can make the change. Luck has nothing to do with it. Get out there and make it happen. Get out there, talk to people, network and make contacts. Enthuse people about yourself or your business. You will be amazed what doors start to open and how quickly your luck starts to change. Let me finish with a true story.

My friend Phil decided to set up a plastering business because he was so disillusioned with his job. He was always quite good with his hands and he went and took a short plastering course.

He set himself up with business cards and tools and started by getting the odd job from family and friends.

One day he came out of his house in Shrewsbury, walked about a hundred metres down the road and noticed that a door to a large house was open. He looked inside the house and saw boxes and all sorts scattered around. He went through the door and, seeing a couple of people standing there, said 'I'm sorry to bother you but I noticed you were moving in. If you need any plastering doing, I only live just up the road and I am sure I could do an excellent job for you.' With that, Phil gave them his business card and left.

A few months went by and Phil got a job with a local builder plastering some barn conversions. Gradually, he became more and more skilled in his work.

We were having a couple of days off work and enjoying the Cheltenham National Hunt festival together when Phil got a call out of the blue.

It was from the owner of the big house in Shrewsbury offering him some work! This was to be his biggest and most lucrative job to date. He was absolutely delighted.

If Phil had not taken the opportunity to walk through that door, he would not have got the job.

He could easily have seen the open door and just kept on walking.

If you don't do, you don't get – in business and in life in general. Luck has nothing to do with it.

Don't feed the ducks...

• Choose a positive attitude

• Make your own luck, make things happen

• Take action. Words are just words –
  without positive action nothing will ever change

• Always back the grey, as my granddad used to say.
  (As I write this, I am thinking about backing a
  wonderful grey horse called Detroit City at the
  Cheltenham Festival. Perhaps there is such a thing as
  luck occasionally? Footnote: Whoops, the grey lost!)

CHAPTER 15

The Ideas Factory

People need to be constantly motivated with new and fresh ideas – innovation is the 'food of life'.

What are the individual ideas and actions that will help you to change the culture of your business and deliver fantastic customer service?

Of course, every organisation is different and every cultural change programme and training experience I create develops new ideas that are appropriate to the particular business I am working with.

I hope that while reading this book you will already have experienced many secrets for creating successful culture change and delivering amazing customer service.

Let me remind you of a couple of really important things here before we go on.

Great customer service starts from the inside out. What's critical is the way people feel about the company they work for. If they are inspired, motivated and proud to work for an organisation, they are more likely to deliver outstanding customer service. People have to believe in what they are doing. Putting it bluntly, they have to want to do it. People need much more than just a wage slip! They need to be constantly inspired and motivated.

> "People... need to be constantly
> inspired and motivated."

One of the best ways you can inspire and motivate your people is to take regular trips to top-performing companies and bring back their ideas to help transform your company. You should set up a programme of visits for employees at all levels. It's a simple idea but, trust me, it really will make a massive difference.

In this chapter, I will share some of the other things that have worked in organisations I have helped. Don't be tempted to believe you can cut corners here and just implement these without doing the other stuff I have talked about in the earlier chapters of this book. Some of these ideas will make a positive impact, but this may be short-lived. You need an all encompassing approach, an ongoing journey to excellence.

Here are some examples to inspire and motivate your people. One organisation I worked with held a children's fun day for its employees. That's **employees**, not customers. It was a beautiful hot July day and over 200 children attended. There was face painting, bouncy castles and food. It didn't cost much money and even people who didn't have children attended. Somebody said to me they had never had such a good day at that particular organisation and they had worked there for years. What a fantastic motivator! The next time somebody wanted them to go the extra mile or to speak positively about the place they worked, they would certainly be more likely to do so.

Let me tell you about the chief executive who, on hearing that people had achieved a particular success or business goal, bought fish and chips for everybody. Or perhaps he would treat them with ice creams or a free bet on the Grand National. He would give whatever matched the occasion, and he would make sure it was seen to be coming personally from him. Of course, he had built an employee reward budget into his financial projections. Again, people appreciate being thanked and rewarded. It really does make a difference.

> "... people appreciate being
> thanked and rewarded.
> It really does make a difference."

Or how about the customer champion who I was working with? Through his own endeavours and effort, he had managed to obtain a 100% return from an employee morale survey during April. He came in early one day and put an Easter egg on everybody's desk. They were surprised and delighted. Do you think they will help him next time he needs them to fill in something? Of course they will, because he has shown them that he and the organisation care.

There is also the company that achieved a superb result at the end of the financial year and sent out their own version of a lottery ticket. On the ticket was a 'thank you' signed from the chief executive and all the directors. The tickets were all individually numbered and were an automatic entry into a prize draw, with the winner having a weekend break for two in a luxury hotel. There were also many other smaller prizes that helped spread the general feel-good factor around the company.

I know one chief executive who, on hearing that the company had achieved a great result on a particular challenge, gave everybody a day off to be taken any time in the next month.

One organisation I've been involved with works in local communities with some very challenging customers. They allocated a dedicated budget to each team and office to design their own relaxing space at the rear of the building. These were called 'living rooms' and each one was different – just like your own living room at home. Individual decoration, televisions, CD players, all intended to make their jobs a little bit more enjoyable. The secret is that the rooms belonged to the teams, and were designed by the teams to be exactly as they wanted. Each one was different but each one also made a huge difference to the quality of the team members' working lives.

How about rewarding people for great ideas? A company set up an 'Amazing Ideas' scheme that offered an extra week's paid holiday for an employee's idea – for their 'Eureka' moment that contributed the most to the success of the company. And on top of the extra week off... an all-expenses-paid holiday for two was thrown in.

I know of several organisations that take corporate responsibility seriously and actively involve employees in raising money for charity or local communities. This means not just collecting money but also everybody taking part in events such as housing estate clear-ups, recycling and working in socially disadvantaged areas. Some organisations even encourage team members to do at least one day a year's work for a local charity or good cause. This can contribute hugely to creating a sense of belief and purpose in their daily work.

Note: the secret here is that you need to keep doing different things to ensure that people do not become complacent. The day off is a really good motivator but perhaps should only be used sparingly and for really brilliant achievements.

I was working closely with a director and his new management team on the importance of praise and reward. We ran a number of sessions with the team and at one point we told everybody that the praise and reward session was a particularly challenging one and would take up the whole of a specified Friday. As lunchtime approached, the director thanked his team for their efforts and hard work in setting up the new systems and promptly gave them the afternoon off and told them to enjoy the weekend. Praise and reward in theory and practice.

There are companies that encourage their employees to come in to work and share their interests and skills with colleagues. Acupuncture, Indian head massage and yoga are a few examples. Some organisations even give people an allowance to experience something new, such as rock climbing or diving. New experiences mean fresh minds and an ability to be creative at work.

> **"New experiences mean fresh minds and an ability to be creative at work."**

A business I know of has its own 'Ministry of Fun' to organise social events, including 'Russian egg roulette' where occasionally managers can literally get egg on their faces.

Many people at my seminars and talks tell me that one of the greatest forms of motivation is a simple, sincere thank you for a good job done. Make an effort to thank people, even diary an hour each week to think about who is performing well and how you can thank them.

And don't forget the partners of the people who work for you. When one great organisation I know of promotes one of its people, it not only congratulates the team member but also sends a gift to their partner as well. And they ask the promoted person what their partner would really like. Can you see how this helps people to form a real connection with the organisation they work with?

Do these things add value to your business? Absolutely! Your people are your most important asset. Take every opportunity to reward them and catch them doing something well. Don't just apply the usual business practice of only telling people when they are doing something badly.

It is worth adding here that internal communication is also one of the greatest motivators. Good consistent feedback and sharing success, both individually and as an organisation, can contribute greatly to improved performance. Encourage managers not to wait until the annual performance review, but to review performance on a daily basis.

I would suggest that you spend some time with a cross-section of employees brainstorming some ways to motivate your people. Create a budget. Give somebody the responsibility for the action, and timetable when it will happen. This is absolutely vital if you are going to create a top-performing company with highly motivated people.

Don't feed the ducks...

- Motivate

- Reward

- Praise

- Innovate

- Inspire!

CHAPTER 16

Hoovers
Really Suck

*Understanding that negative,
demotivated people can kill your
business stone dead!*

I would like to spend a little bit of time talking to you now about recruiting the right people with the right attitude and personality. If we are going to continue our journey towards creating a successful culture and fantastic customer service, this is absolutely essential.

Every time a new employee walks through the door of your business, it is an opportunity to move things forward. It is a chance to bring somebody in to help you out, to make life easier for your colleagues and your customers. If you get it wrong, however, and employ the wrong person, you can end up with a millstone around your neck that drags you and your business down and down. We are not very good at addressing poor performance and sorting out problems with people, so it makes sense to get it right first time.

I need to recap here on the previous chapter, 'Choose your Attitude'. Is there a barrier to your choosing a positive attitude? What can stop you being positive? Do you know certain people at work who make you feel good just by having a chat with them – who energise you just by the way they are? These people are great to be around. Whenever you can, at home or at work, surround yourself with positive people. They make life and business much easier. On the other hand, do you also know certain characters at work who I like to describe as the 'Mood Hoovers'? Let me explain a little bit more…

"Whenever you can, at home or at work, surround yourself with positive people."

It is 8.30 in the morning. You are feeling really good about things. Life is good, you have chosen a positive attitude and you are actually looking forward to the challenges that the day will bring.

Then suddenly, as you walk through the door of your office, you meet him, the Mood Hoover. By 8.31 he has sucked all the positive energy out of you and you are a lifeless, negative wreck, unable to bring any positive thought to the day. Now, be honest with yourself, have you got any of these at work? It gets worse, though.

After many years of hoovering their way through the positive culture you are desperately trying to create, they finish their Degree in Negativity and start to form a little group of moaners. These are even worse, and I like to call them the Destructive Dysons, happily sucking away for all their worth. (The term 'Destructive Dysons' is used here to describe a negative type and is no way intended as a criticism of the superb products manufactured by the Dyson company.) You know the types I mean. They love you to fail. If there isn't any bad news, they will sit in little rooms somewhere making it up. For example, the company is going bust, there will be no pay rise this year, somebody has got promoted who doesn't deserve it, the management are taking the p**s, so and so has been sacked unfairly, the chief executive is earning more than Robbie Williams, it is a rubbish company to work for, and so on…

The problem is that by now they have become absolutely brilliant at destroying your reputation. They tell your customers what a terrible place your company is to work and how badly they are treated. They even tell their friends and family, for God's sake. Their negativity will grind your business into the ground. They love you to fail, they really do.

Eventually, after many years of hoovering away, a terrible thing can happen and they are promoted beyond their ability. They become what I like to call the 'negative leaders'! They confidently walk through the corridors proclaiming proudly to everybody who will listen that this is a crap place to work and laughing manically to themselves in their office about the sheer awfulness and madness of it all.

Do you know one of these? Granted, there are only a few of these characters in every organisation. They are a unique species, if you like. But, boy, are they good at what they do! These negative leaders are assassins and internal terrorists who will kill your business from the inside out. I am not talking about the people who have a moan and move on. We all like to moan about something: love, life, the neighbours, next door's dog, and so on. That is normal. But when you have had your moan, as the fantastic speaker Paul McGee would say, just SUMO – Shut Up and Move On (see Bibliography.) Life is too short.

You can probably tell that I have come across a number of these characters. In some ways, they are strange motivators for me. They make me really want to try to improve businesses just to shut them up. There are always a few of them in every business. Do not underestimate them, they are very dangerous.

Now you could say here that perhaps I am being a little harsh. Perhaps it really is a crap place to work, perhaps all the terrible things they say are true. That's ok if they are trying their best to change things, to knock some barriers down, to improve things for colleagues, to improve things for customers even. But they never do, they just don't. All they love to do is moan and try to bring everybody down with them.

If we are lucky, sometimes they decide that the place is now far too successful and they go and work somewhere else. However, we are on the road to creating a fantastically successful company here. So please, do yourself a favour and unplug the bloody Mood Hoovers! Sack them, encourage them to see the errors of their ways, religiously convert them if needs be, but make sure when the time is right you move them on. Most people just want to do a good job and be fairly rewarded. Most people can be influenced, though.

Make sure they are being influenced by your passionate, positive people and not by your moaners.

> "Make sure your people are being influenced by your passionate, positive people and not by your moaners."

Sometimes Mood Hoovers don't know that that's what they are. I heard a true story about somebody who, after attending one of my launch events, went up to his boss and said 'Ralph, am I really a Hoover? I am, aren't I?' Ralph replied 'Yes, sometimes.' Ever since that day, Ralph has told me that the man has been completely transformed. He used to be totally negative and bring everybody around him down to his level. He is a different person now and brings a positive attitude to work, sometimes even inspiring his colleagues as well.

Don't feed the ducks...

- Unplug the Mood Hoovers

- Inspire or fire

- SUMO – Shut up and move on!

CHAPTER 17

Positive People Make the Difference, They Really Do!

Recruit for attitude and surround yourself with positive people who can help you achieve your aims.

Positive people make the difference, they really do. If I had to suggest one thing and one thing only that can transform your business, it would be that you recruit great people with a brilliant attitude. Surround yourself with positive people.

> "If I had to suggest one thing and one thing only that can transform your business, it would be that you recruit great people with a brilliant attitude."

I once attended a business conference and had the pleasure of listening to a very interesting speaker called John Seddon. He was a disciple of the Toyota way with a belief in lean thinking and robust systems, known as Kaizen, the Japanese term for continuous improvement.

I can recommend that you read John's book if you have an interest in improving systems and cutting out waste. He is totally dedicated to improving systems and really believes if you get that right everything else looks after itself.

But after listening to him, I thought to myself 'What comes first, the people or the systems?' For me, every time, it is the people. Without the people, you can't create the systems; without motivated people, you can't get them to carry out the systems with any pride or urgency; and, finally, without people who really believe in what they are doing, you will not deliver brilliant face-to-face customer service.

Granted, you need excellent systems but you also definitely need excellent people.

Without exception, every truly successful organisation employs motivated people with a positive attitude towards colleagues and customers. This doesn't just happen by accident: these organisations make a concerted effort to ensure they employ the right people. They actively recruit for attitude or personality.

> ## "Without exception, every truly successful organisation employs motivated people with a positive attitude towards colleagues and customers."

There are many sceptics out there who don't believe in it, can't understand it or just think it is wishy-washy rubbish, powder-puff thinking or just plain stupid. I can guarantee that, if they feel like that, they are at this very minute working for an underachieving or average organisation.

It is not difficult to recruit great people. Take a leaf through one of my bibles, *The Sunday Times 100 Best Companies to Work For*, and you will find many examples of companies that put this as a foundation of their business strategy.

"It is not difficult to recruit great people."

I was working with an organisation that was dedicated to employing some brilliant people for the opening of their new call centre. This is a brief story of the recruiting-for-attitude process we went through.

There were 80 people attending the sessions on a Saturday morning. Each session had about 25 people in it and lasted for about an hour. They were all asked to dress casually.

The attitude assessment started immediately they entered the room. Each candidate was asked to put on a name badge and was handed a questionnaire. The questionnaire asked them to find somebody they had never met before and answer the questions on the sheet.

What they didn't know was that, while they were doing this, they were being closely watched by a number of observers. Each observer had three specific people to view for their attitude and behaviour.

We had created a simple tick sheet that the observers were asked to fill in and rate the candidates on a scale of one to five. The categories were fun, connection, positivity, energy and passion. Without going into too much detail here, the assessors were looking for people who actually engaged with each other, smiled, listened and showed a little bit of interest in what was happening around them. People who liked people.

I then facilitated a number of group activities with them to see how they interacted with each other. I am not talking about building a raft with an egg box and a toilet roll here. I was asking them to engage in conversations and give some answers, such as 'What are you passionate about in life, what motivates you, who inspires you?' This is the key thing really – to find out how people get on with others. You can tell an enormous amount about someone just by observing his or her behaviour.

> "You can tell an enormous amount
> about someone just by observing
> his or her behaviour."

It was interesting to hear afterwards that the observers found it really easy to quickly spot the people who would not be suitable to join the organisation and rule them out. These were the people who didn't talk to each other, smile or show any interest at all.

Afterwards the successful people were shortlisted and invited back for the more traditional interview, which looked in more depth at skills, qualifications and general suitability for the job in question. The important thing here, though, is that everybody, without exception, who had been shortlisted for interview had specifically been selected for his or her attitude. They already displayed certain qualities. They were a certain type of positive person. Again the assessors said that at interview, because of the recruitment-for-attitude session, they felt that they already knew the people, which made it easier to select the best people for the job.

Now, I know this is all subjective and it is really important that the observers' criteria match the values of the organisation. But, at the end of the day, it is your business. No matter how large or small you are, it is essential to recruit the right people. If you only had one person working for you in your business 'Squeaky Clean Windows Ltd', you would ensure that you employed the right person, wouldn't you? Somebody who would treat customers well, smile occasionally, take some pride in what they do and actually clean some windows.

> "No matter how large or small you are, it is essential to recruit the right people."

I put it to you that you just cannot afford to recruit the wrong type of person. Your company can't afford it, you would underperform and you would go out of business. It is no different for your business, large or small. People make the difference.

"People make the difference."

There are a couple of final points here. Number one, this can't happen in isolation. It has to be part of a larger programme to change the culture of your business. Number two, it is up to you! At the end of the day, you live or die by the people you employ. Many failing businesses pay little or no attention to the recruitment of people with the right personalities and attitude to make their business a success. This is summed up brilliantly in *The One Minute Manager* by Ken Blanchard. First of all, try to recruit the best people. Secondly, recruit people with potential and train them well. If you can't do these things, you might as well put your hands together and pray.

"At the end of the day, you live or die by the people you employ."

Don't feed the ducks...

• Recruit for attitude

• Hire for personality

• Pay great attention to your recruitment process

CHAPTER 18

Forgive us our Sins!

How not to motivate and inspire your people!

We the willing
Led by the unknowing
Doing the impossible
For the ungrateful
We have now done so much
For so long – for so many
With so little
We can now do anything
With nothing!

[Anonymous, seen on a sign in Bowness-on-Windemere, Cumbria]

As a lapsed Catholic, I understand clearly the need to repent for our many sins. There are many businesses out there that also should hang their heads in shame with guilt for the many terrible deeds that they have inflicted on their employees.

There are a number of useful lessons that can be learnt from these terrible crimes and, to be honest, a lot of laughs as well.

I have deliberately made this a short chapter as I think the message is very clear. To protect the innocent and avoid being sued, I will not name the businesses concerned here. Their sheer incompetence rivals even that of the board of my local football club. How people can be treated so badly completely baffles me. And yet these incompetent so-called leaders expect their people to deliver fantastic service, work long hours and show incredible loyalty. It just doesn't work like that, and it is no wonder that they will probably go out of business or always completely underperform.

Let me introduce you first to an employee who told me that, having worked for a council for four weeks and despite several requests, they hadn't even been given the keys to their own office. Of course there would be the usual excuses – it's not their fault, it's down to human resources or the janitor or whatever. Why not just give them the bloody keys?

Or how about the organisation that, in the interests of motivation and rewarding their employees, gave out a special award for people who arrived on time every day and did not miss a day at work through sickness. However, even if you were thirty seconds late, it meant that you were penalised and your whole team were as well!

The splendid reward for achievement of these targets was a pizza party and an extra half-hour lunch. We are talking about a multi-million pound company here and all they could do is buy their people a pizza! The idea of reward is good but they did more long-term damage to employee relations than good. I wonder if they allowed them extra cheese topping?!

Amazingly enough, the managing director would get really upset when people used to get up and leave right on the dot at five o'clock each night at home time. It was pointed out to him that, because people were treated in such a childish way over their timekeeping at the start of the day, it was unlikely that they were going to give anything back at the other end. He just stared blankly. He didn't have the faintest idea how to motivate and inspire his people. I was later told that one frustrated and browbeaten employee was witnessed telling this leader to stick his pizza party where the sun doesn't shine.

I heard of one leader who banned all office Christmas parties on religious grounds. A sure-fire way to inspire your people and build commitment if ever I heard it. Not! What about the boss who was so inflexible that he would fine people for even being a couple of minutes late after lunch? They used the heart-warming phrase: '45 minutes is 45 minutes, not a minute more'!

I have a really good friend called Phil who has told me a number of horror stories concerning one particular business he worked for. Actually there is a really positive outcome to this story. Phil was so unhappy at this place that he has now started his own very successful business (see the 'Luck of the Irish' chapter).

Occasionally Phil can be heard manically chanting his favourite mantra: 'I'm not at Deesley Motors, I'm not at Deesley Motors, I'm not at Deesley Motors', while rocking rhythmically from side to side. (To protect the guilty, the name of the company Phil worked for has been changed to the utterly fictional 'Deesley Motors'.)

He honestly does this every time things might get a bit hard in his new business, or if he ever has to ask himself if he has made the right decision to go self-employed. The mantra reminds him that nothing could be as bad as working for Deesley Motors, **nothing**.

I'll explain.

The boss would be on the shop floor and notice a colleague entering Phil's department. Within a minute, he would burst in and demand that they stop 'chatting'. By his intimidating style, the boss would make the other person feel like a powerless child.

The environment was so oppressive that it was impossible for people to even talk about work matters without feeling guilty or judged.

It was so bad that employees were worried that the staff canteen, shop floor and the offices were bugged and they were being constantly listened to. This might not sound so paranoid when you know that actually all departments were monitored by CCTV.

I have talked earlier about creating a fun environment to work where people could have a laugh. At Deesley, all communication was crushed. Work, work, work, don't talk, don't think, just do! It was like working at a prison camp, but the employees weren't the ones with the guns. Phil told me that there were good people there who didn't deserve that sort of treatment. He was aware that the potential was huge if only the manager had the faintest idea of the power of motivating, rewarding and inspiring the people.

I would like to finish this tale with a reminder that, when things get tough, it is worth appreciating what you have in life and work.

Phil recently received a phone call from somebody he used to work with at Deesley Motors. He told him that the atmosphere was even worse. People were leaving and that he was desperately looking for another job. Phil had made the move. He had done something about his situation. Life is too short; take action to change things.

> "Life is too short;
> take action to change things."

When Phil put the phone down he could be heard quietly chanting to himself 'I'm not at Deesley Motors, I'm not at Deesley Motors, I'm not at Deesley Motors'...

Don't feed the ducks...

- Never work at 'Deesley Motors' –
  if you do, leave as soon as you can!

CHAPTER 19

Drive Your Cars One Way Around the Track

The importance of creating a strong external brand.

When I was 16 and had just finished my CSEs and O levels, I thought it might be a good idea to do something different during the summer holidays and hitch-hike round the country with my best mate Guy. We had very little money and no idea where we would end up, but we set off with £10, to last us six weeks, a tent and loads of youthful enthusiasm.

The first day we walked and hitched and found ourselves an amazing 190 miles from home. Everything was brilliant. There we were, away from our parents with the excitement of not knowing what we would get up to. Then it started to rain, and rain and rain. We found ourselves on the top of a hill, in a leaking tent, sitting in an ever-increasing pool of water. We were cold, miserable and had no food.

After a few days of endless rain, sleeping in service stations and surviving on a daily diet of bread and biscuits, we decided we had to do something about it. One thing was certain: we were definitely not going to admit defeat and go home to our parents with our tails between our legs.

> "One thing was certain: we were definitely not going to admit defeat and go home to our parents with our tails between our legs."

I remembered that my mom and stepdad, Roy, used to take me to Barmouth in North Wales for caravan holidays in the summer. There used to be two fairgrounds there, one at each end of the sea front. It was simple. We would make our way to Barmouth and get a job working on the fair.

After a tiring day hitching our way to Barmouth, we finally arrived. It was pitch black and tipping it down with rain. We decided to try and stay dry by standing by the side of the dodgems. Suddenly, out of the gloom, loomed a giant of a man who asked us what we were doing.

> "Suddenly, out of the gloom, loomed a giant of a man who asked us what we were doing."

We told him our story and he took pity on us and said that we could sleep that night under the cover of the dodgems. He said that if anybody bothered us we should just tell them that, 'Walter said it would be alright.'

We were so tired that we fell straight to sleep. Then, suddenly, we were woken by a bloke angrily shouting at us, 'What the hell are you doing in there?' Quick as lightning we said, 'Walter said that it would be alright.' And sure enough it worked its magic because Bronco, as we later found out he was called, stopped shouting and even invited us into his trailer for a cup of tea and some biscuits.

The next day, we asked Walter for a job and we got one working on the dodgems and other fairground rides. I ended up working there for the rest of the summer and for the next two summers as well.

During my time there I really grew up and learnt a lot of lessons about life in general. Walter became a sort of father figure to me and there was one thing that really stood out about him. He had a passion for his family, his business and life in general.

> "There was one thing that really stood out about him.
> He had a passion for his family, his business and life in general."

He owned the fairground and always made sure that it looked its best and was clean and tidy. Every morning it was our job to sweep the grounds from end to end and clean the rides and the dodgems. Walter was intensely proud of his business and he wouldn't let anyone or anything damage it.

One of the things I really enjoyed was speaking over the microphone on the dodgems when the music was playing. Notice, I used the word 'dodgems' not 'bumper cars'. That was because if someone bumped a car head on it could be damaged and the car could be out of action for a day or two. I know this doesn't sound much but, in the peak season when the track was busy every day, a car off the track could mean losing a considerable amount of money from the 'punters'.

My favourite saying that I used to boom over the speakers was 'It's a long ride, it's a fast ride and if you fall out it's your last ride. Drive your cars one way around the track and one way only.'

> ## "It's a long ride, it's a fast ride and if you fall out it's your last ride. Drive your cars one way around the track and one way only."

Now at times of great stress or pressure in my life I sometimes say 'It's a long ride, it's a fast ride and if you fall out it's your last ride. Drive your cars one way around the track and one way only.'

If any poor punter was stupid enough to ignore this instruction and smash head on to another car, he would be unscrupulously ejected from the track and booted off the fairground by Walter, Bronco or his son Jason.

In many ways, there was always a hint of danger or violence at the fair. Now you could not get anybody more opposed to violence than me. At the time, I was happiest when I was writing songs or poetry. I suppose I could be cheeky though and one day I learnt a lesson that stayed with me for the rest of my life.

I was a bit cheeky to Jason and had a bit of a mood on me that day. He chased me all the way to my room and knocked me down on the floor, grabbed my throat and, red in the face with anger and his fist tightly clenched, screamed in my face, 'Never take liberties with people who are trying to help you, never!' He didn't hit me. He just left me on the floor.

After that, I didn't ever cheek him again. He never touched me again as long as I worked there and we became good friends.

In business, to be a success you have to be passionate about what you do. You need to always learn from your mistakes, just as I did with Jason. You have to have good people around you and treat them with the respect they deserve. Walter certainly had good people around him and in some ways you could say he was lucky because he had a ready-made team in his family. But he still had to inspire them with his vision and passion for the business.

They were really hard working and determined to be successful.

"You have to have good people around you and treat them with the respect they deserve."

I'm not sure if this is true but I was told that Walter was three quarters of the way to his first million when I was working for him. Knowing Walter and his family, it was easy to see why.

Walter once told me one of his business secrets. What made him his real money wasn't the dodgems or the other rides with the bright flashing lights, loud music and excitement. These were what he called the 'flash' – the things that attracted people onto the fairground. He wanted them to have a go on the dodgems, yes, but what he really wanted was for them to spend money in his arcade on the slot machines. That was where the real money was to be made, but he had to get them interested in the first place.

So think about your business for a second here. You can have the best business, the most fantastic people and product but if you can't get the people through the door you will fail.

So what is your 'flash', the thing that will attract people to your business? Have a look at my website if you like, www. liamoconnell.co.uk, and see if I have really learnt this important lesson from Walter. I suppose you could say that my ducks are my 'flash' and you would be right.

I believe that image is incredibly important. I couldn't believe it when a solicitor opened up a new office in my home town of Shifnal. For the first two weeks, they had a pathetic, amateurish sign above the door that showed the fading and peeling paint in the space where the old sign used to be.

What does it say to the potential customer? Is this a professional business, somebody I can trust to help me out with some serious issues, or just a shoddy, can't-be-bothered, two-bit outfit? I think you get the picture.

Just like David Birkett, in the '**it Happens' chapter, if you create a vibrant imaginative image, it says something about you and your business to your customers. I can never understand people who underestimate this side of running a successful business. They always say something like 'I can't afford to spend money on that type of thing,' or 'I will get around to it later.' Later never happens.

> "... if you create a vibrant
> imaginative image, it says something
> about you and your business
> to your customers."

So anyway, it's a long ride, it's a fast ride...

Another great example of image making is my friend Sal, who decided to set up a new hairdressing business. Sal didn't just go for the usual corny 'a cut above the rest' or 'chopping block' approach. That is not only patronising, it just doesn't work. She called it 'Spirit', a name that stands out, that

makes people think. It evokes a feeling of more than just a
new hairstyle or a particular cut. It goes to the very essence of
creating a memorable and enjoyable experience for customers.
Sal has created a brand that reflects her intention to enhance
someone's lifestyle. It has worked and Spirit is incredibly
successful.

I suppose I have always wanted to do things that are
different. I didn't know when I set off hitch-hiking that I
would grow up and my life would change on a fairground in
Barmouth. I didn't know that for the first time in my life I
would earn some really good money and live independently. I
changed my hairstyle while I was there and Guy even
changed his name to Sid. He is still called that today.

We met some brilliant people but the one outstanding
memory is Walter and his passion for his fairground, his
business. He had intense pride in what he did and he was
very successful.

In my last week working with Walter, he offered me the
chance to buy a fairground ride and stay there permanently
working with him. I turned him down, I often wondered
what would have happened if I had taken him up on his
offer…

Don't feed the ducks...

- Inspire people with your passion – it is infectious

- Treat people with the respect they deserve

- Find your own 'flash' to stand out from the crowd

- It's a long ride, it's a fast ride, if you fall out it's your last ride

CHAPTER 20

No Ducks

Understand that
great customer service starts
with your people –
from the inside out.

So this is where the ducks come in. Those ducks, those little yellow plastic ducks! What a massive part they have played in my life. I think I need to explain.

When I first started getting into customer service and culture change a number of years ago, I decided I needed to learn from some of the best providers of customer service in the country. One of the first companies that came to mind was Asda. They pride themselves on delivering brilliant customer service with a fun culture and great people. They are in one of the most competitive industries in the world and continually compete with Tesco, Sainsburys, Waitrose and others in an ongoing series of what can only be described as Supermarket Wars.

I began working with a customer services manager in my local Asda store. I learnt an enormous amount from him about service and what makes a really successful organisation tick.

By the way, did you know that at one point in its history Asda had a terrible reputation for service and were only a few weeks away from going bust? Then Archie Norman took over and everything changed. Yes, he wanted increased profits. Yes, he wanted brilliant customer service. And above all, he wanted to be a success. But he started from the inside out; he started with his people. He motivated them, he gave them direction and flexible working, and he rewarded them for their efforts. He created a fun place to work with people who actually like people.

Asda always recruit for attitude and personality and put an enormous amount of time and money into the process to ensure they recruit lively, friendly people with a great attitude to work.

Archie Norman created a people- and customer-driven organisation with strong community involvement. His success led to Asda being second only to Tesco in sales. They were taken over by Wallmart, who were so impressed with the positive culture already in place that they kept the same values.

The Asda success story proves that, without doubt, these things work. Some people say that attitude, direction and motivation are fluffy notions with no substance. I beg to differ. The results speak for themselves.

Asda invited me to attend an induction session for new starters on a Saturday morning. There we were, all in our green branded polo shirts. Then suddenly the trainer said 'Congratulations, you have already done really well to get here. We don't just employ anybody at Asda, we want a certain type of person with a great attitude.' Then he said it. 'We don't have ducks working at Asda… we have eagles.'

> ### "We don't just employ anybody... we want a certain type of person with a great attitude."

What he meant was that they employed passionate people, who were passionate about their work and colleagues. People who like people. They didn't want ducks because they display a certain type of negative behaviour. So what negative phrases might you associate with ducks?

- It is water off a duck's back

- You get nothing for a duck in cricket

- Follow blindly one after another

- Duck the issues

- More interested in policies and procedures than in people

- Ducking and diving

- Grumble and squabble

- Dead duck

I think you have probably got the idea now. Somebody even told me to 'duck off' recently, although I have no idea what he meant! Anyway the point is that, if you want to create a successful business, you need to surround yourself with passionate people who can think for themselves. Not individuals who can't be bothered, continually moaning and being miserable. You know what I mean – the people whose biggest success every day is just getting up in the morning. We don't want ducks working in our organisations. Great service starts with the people, from the inside out. (Let me tell you a little secret. I love ducks actually, but not in the workplace!)

The next time you experience terrible customer service, and feel helpless or even humiliated, I want you to do something for me. Imagine the person right in front of you is a giant duck. Go on, do it. Have a good laugh to yourself at their terrible attitude and complete indifference to the reality of the situation.

> "The next time you experience
> terrible customer service...
> imagine the person right in front of you
> is a giant duck."

Let me give you an example. My wife Sue and I decided that we would go for a long weekend in Chester. The only problem was that we couldn't stay for three nights in our favourite hotel because it was full. So we had to spend one night in a different hotel and two nights in our normal one.

So there we were, happy as Larry and looking forward to a weekend away. We walked into the lobby merrily dragging our suitcase on wheels behind us and then we saw it.

Right in front of us was a giant duck sitting at the reception desk. She was miserable, frowning, down, couldn't even be bothered to say hello. We might as well have turned around and gone straight home. As usual, I could smell the culture!

Suddenly she got up without saying anything and disappeared into this little room next to reception. Have you seen those little rooms? Goodness knows what they do in there! So there we were, left stranded and helpless. What a welcome!

Was this person just having a bad day? Did she have a bad attitude in general or could she just not be bothered? Or was it because she had no idea what she was doing there, she was given no direction, motivation or reward or any feeling that she was part of something successful? I think I know the

answer. Wherever I went that night, I saw duck after duck
after duck. All aimlessly following negatively one after
another. It was like a virus; bird flu had spread throughout
the business.

The next day, we were happy to check out and move to the
next hotel. There we were... suitcase on wheels, walking
through the lobby. Then we saw her, a passionate person,
smiling, warm and friendly. This was not a product of a
customer service course but a genuine person who really
wanted to help us. What a difference! And then just as she
was giving us the keys to our room, she gave us a map of
Chester and said 'Perhaps this might help you while you are
here.' Brilliant! Fantastic!

So why can't every organisation do it? It's not difficult, is it?
This person had a real pride in her job and organisation. And
that is the key to creating a successful, service-orientated
organisation. Instilling pride and purpose in your people.
Don't feed the ducks, the negative people. Inspire your
people, create a brilliant business.

> "Don't feed the ducks,
> the negative people.
> Inspire your people, create a brilliant
> business."

From there on in, the duck stuff just went mad. I wanted to think of something fresh and different for a new speech. And I started throwing ducks of all shapes, colours and sizes into the audience at the start of my talks. People were immediately interested. It was fun, there was a real energy in the room. People liked what I was doing. It was entertaining yet had a strong message that was linked to the importance of inspiring people. The word began to spread, my business began to take off and is still rapidly expanding today. I have never had to advertise to get work. It has all come from word of mouth – the best form of public relations. I am not resting on my laurels, though. I want to take my positive message to as many organisations and people as possible. I still have big ideas and dreams. If you think big, the obstacles are tiny by comparison.

From one simple idea I created a strong successful brand, Don't feed the ducks…It was just an idea that worked. All my life I have had ideas and tried different things, some worked and some didn't, but the important thing was that I remembered that my mom told me to never ever give up! I am still trying and if you like this book you might want to try my new one *My Fire's Gone Out*, it's about coping with change and keeping your personal motivation, your fire if you like, burning.

I have now also developed my own "no duck" philosophy, perhaps you would like to have a go at answering the questions below.

- Can you focus on what is important?

- Do you believe you will succeed?

- Can you choose your mood?

- Do you appreciate the people around you?

- Do you recognise opportunities and take action?

- Do you sometimes step out of your comfort zone?

- What will be your legacy in life?

I have also come across many different ducks since I originally wrote this book, remember whatever you do don't feed the ducks in your business or your life!

Mood Hoover   Negative Leader   Destructive Dyson

Assassin   Victim   Envy   Bully

(The term 'Destructive Dysons' is used here to describe a negative type and is no way intended as a criticism of the superb products manufactured by the Dyson company.)

Don't feed the ducks...

- Employ passionate people, people who like people

- Create great service from the inside out

- Learn from the best

- Don't give up... Find your own ducks

CHAPTER 21

The Taste
of Darcy's

*A brilliant real-life example of
how commitment and a passion
for people can bring you successes.*

You have no chance opening a restaurant here: there are too many already, far too much competition. If I were you, I would try somewhere else.'

These were the 'positive' words of encouragement that greeted Jim Morrison from some of the local business owners when he decided to open Darcy's Trattoria, a new restaurant in the Shropshire town of Shifnal.

Jim was determined to prove the doubters wrong. Let me ask you a question? How many restaurants do you know that have people regularly queuing for a table at six o'clock in the evening? Jim's place does all the time.

Darcy's Trattoria is fantastically successful and incredibly busy. When you visit you will notice a fun, happening atmosphere almost like a party, brilliant food and it will be packed with happy loyal customers.

> "... you will notice a fun, happening atmosphere almost like a party..."

There are some incredibly good lessons that we can learn from Jim and adapt to any business. It doesn't matter what the industry is. At the end of the day, it is the standard of service you deliver and the people that make the difference.

There are a number of points in this chapter that summarise some of the strong themes running throughout this book.

This is Jim's story.

Jim puts the customer at the heart of everything he does. Without them you go out of business. 'No customers' means 'no business'. Simple.

> *'We never need to advertise. If you get it right your reputation will sell it for you. People are often turned away because we are full or the waiting time is too long. Some people might see this as a negative thing but I think it just increases our reputation. If it is busy, it must be good. If you can't have something, you want it more. People really make the effort and come early to make sure they get a table next time.'*

He is an incredibly friendly and warm host and always finds time to chat to his customers. He doesn't walk around sucking up to people, like so many others, who as he says 'are really up themselves'. He is always seen behind his counter, working hard and creating an energy and vibrancy that spreads throughout the restaurant.

'At the end of the day it is all about people. We don't give any formal customer care training to our employees. We just make sure that we employ them for their attitude. We want people who have real passion and pride for the business. People who are self-motivated and enjoy working here.

'I don't want people coming into work with the "Oh s**t factor" and saying, "What the hell am I doing here?" I want people to feel good, enjoy their work and in turn make the customers feel good as well. We look after our people, pay good wages and often go out for meals or celebrations as a team.'

There are a number of things that have enabled Jim's business to be successful. The ingredients for success are:

- Good quality food

- Value for money

- Excellent location

- Great atmosphere and environment

- Brilliant people

- Excellent customer service experience

Many of the things listed here are common sense. But how many people really make the effort to do them all properly? Jim says the reason that so many businesses fail is that they do one or two things very well but then ignore some of the others. To be successful, you have to do them all well.

However, Jim's main ingredient for success is delivering an excellent customer service experience.

'I always encourage our team of employees to make a conscious effort to make a connection with the customer. Every time you make a positive connection with a customer, you are building the reputation of your business. If people recognise somebody, I want them to let them know they know them. It doesn't even matter if you can't remember their names; it makes people feel special and valued as customers.

'It is important to break down the barriers. Talk to them about something other than the food. Talk about the weather if necessary. People are not machines, they want to engage with you. After all, they have come out for a good, relaxed experience. Be a real person, be interesting and interested.

'I always tell people it is not about the "smile and have a nice day" forced approach; it is about being yourself and doing what comes naturally. We have

customers from all backgrounds coming in here, but they all want to be treated with respect and have an enjoyable experience. You can also tell very quickly when people want to be quiet or alone. Whatever the person or the situation, a smile costs nothing.'

Every night they have somebody dedicated to welcoming people to Darcy's, called the 'seaty greety'. They sit people down, explain how to order, where the specials board is, make them feel at home and finally say goodbye.

'At the end of the night, I want people to leave with a great taste in their mouth. Not just a fabulous last cup of coffee, but the feeling they get when they go out of the door.'

Jim insists that he and his staff make every effort to say thanks, good night or have a good weekend. This final small genuine human gesture makes all the difference to the overall experience.

Darcy's is an incredibly successful business. There are many lessons that we can learn from Jim. Anybody can do it, you just need determination, passion and a clear understanding of the importance of working with great people who share your ambition.

Darcy's is not a cold, impersonal name. It is a reflection of real people providing a great experience and customers having a fantastic time and enjoying the food. I am going to let Jim have the final words here.

'I love what I do, I count my customers as friends. When I wake up one morning and think to myself that I am not happy any more, or I don't want to be here, that is the time to do something different with my life.'

"Anybody can do it, you just need determination, passion and a clear understanding of the importance of working with great people who share your ambition."

Don't feed the ducks...

• Create a fantastic service experience

• Make a genuine connection with people

• Be interesting and interested

• Remember: no customers = no business

• A bottle of full-bodied red, please, Jim

CHAPTER 22

Let Me Entertain You

*Connecting with
your people and your customers
can give you a
real competitive advantage.*

As I sang the final words of the song, Alex Vann's hypnotic piano playing seemed to have cast a spell on the audience. The nursery-rhyme-like tune began to fade and I started handing out large red balloons to the front row of the crowd. Everybody seemed lost in the surreal moment as the balloons floated at the front of the audience. As we left the stage, the applause was ringing in our ears. It had been a fantastic night, a great show.

I was performing a gig at Birmingham Ronnie Scott's club in front of about 400 people in a packed-out venue.

I have always loved entertaining – from the age of about five when, at a birthday party, my mom picked me up and put me on a seat to sing congratulations to the host of the party – right up to the current day as a professional speaker. There is something inside me that loves being on stage. Perhaps it is something to do with my difficult early childhood and is a subconscious search for recognition and acceptance. I'm not sure, but for me there is nothing like seeing an audience moved by my songs or my performance.

The first time that I realised that I wanted to be a performer was when I saw The Jam at Wolverhampton Civic Hall. Paul Weller's father, John, introduced them with the words, 'Are you ready for the best f***ing band in the world, The Jam!' From the minute Weller struck the first power chord on his guitar, the crowd went absolutely crazy.

His energy, passion and belief made an impression that night that has lasted for the rest of my life.

I am really passionate about what I do and believe that, if you are passionate about something, you can make an amazing connection with any audience.

> "I am really passionate about what I do
> and believe that, if you are passionate
> about something, you can make an
> amazing connection with any audience."

Connection is the key word here and I believe that connection can also be incredibly important in any culture change project or customer service initiative. I like to call this the Three Points of Connection. It is very powerful.

THREE POINTS OF CONNECTION

The
FIRST POINT OF CONNECTION
is

'THE COMPANY AND YOU'

This is the way a company connects
with its people. Does it create a place
where people want to come to work,
feel valued and understand what they
are contributing to? Does it motivate people to
deliver fantastic customer service.
Does it promote a sense of loyalty
and commitment?

The
SECOND POINT OF CONNECTION
is

'YOU AND EACH OTHER'

Great customer service starts
from the inside out.
It is the way people connect with each other.
Helping people out, going the extra mile
for a colleague not just a customer.
Business is often challenging,
so why not try and make it easier
for you and your colleagues?

The
THIRD POINT OF CONNECTION
is

'YOU AND YOUR CUSTOMERS'

Every time you make a connection with
a customer, it is an opportunity to enhance
your reputation as a brilliant organisation.
It is the chance to make an emotional bond
with a customer and create
a magic moment.
It is a chance to move your organisation
from good to fantastic.
Remember: 'no customers' means
'no business'!

In 2005, I was taking part in a fund-raising concert for the Tsunami disaster fund. It had been a brilliant night with various bands performing. I was excited and nervous but I took the attitude that I was going to go out there and make a massive connection with the audience. By the end of my final song, I had unplugged my guitar and was holding it over my head while the crowd sang the words over and over again. It was a magic feeling, I had made a massive connection with the people and, more importantly, we had raised thousands of pounds for charity.

I never quite made it as a professional singer or songwriter with Leven Creed, one of my bands, or with Alex Vann in our duo Vann/O'Connell, but I certainly had fun trying. I have worked with many talented musicians. I had various skirmishes with record companies, including Polydor, and recorded a number of CDs, including one that was produced by The Beautiful South's producer John Brough.

For one reason or another, it was just not to be. But little did I know that, a few years later, all that time on stage playing to different audiences and the work that I put into trying to make it in the music business would help me become a successful professional speaker.

I had spent a lot of money and many hours chasing my dream to be a successful singer songwriter. It had played a massive part in my life. But the time wasn't wasted. A few years ago when I was singing and had the aim of making it in the music business, I had no idea that it would lead me to what I do today, sitting here writing my book and regularly speaking and performing across the country. I now fully understand the power of making an emotional connection with people. As I said in an earlier chapter, you make your own luck in life. If you believe in something and keep trying, keep pushing, eventually something positive will happen.

> "I now fully understand the power of making an emotional connection with people."

I really believe in my business and what I speak about. If I didn't, people would see straight through me. You can tell when a musician is just going through the motions or when a speaker is about as interesting as watching paint dry. Great singers, actors and speakers all have the ability to make a passionate connection with their audience. My passion is to try to improve people's businesses and help change their lives.

I love what I do. I am still growing, trying to improve and learning different things. I am not content with what I have achieved; I am still restless, still searching.

> "If you believe in something and keep trying, keep pushing, eventually something positive will happen."

The same thing applies in business. If you have belief and passion in what you do, it positively enthuses and motivates the people around you. I am continually amazed by people who think that they will be a success at work or in their private life by just going through the motions – people who think that average is good enough. Average quickly becomes poor and poor soon leads to failure.

> "Average quickly becomes poor and poor soon leads to failure."

Are you really happy in your work? Do you get up most days and think to yourself 'I really love my job and I am looking forward to going in to the office today'? A couple of years ago, in the book *Good to Great* by Jim Collins, I came across something that really helped me to focus on what I wanted out of life, what I like to call my 'one big thing'.

The following paraphrases this.

Ask yourself these three questions.

- What are you passionate about in life?

- What are you really good at and could possibly be the best at?

- Can you make money from doing it?

Many very successful companies and people continually ask themselves these questions. Sometimes it can takes months, or even years to come up with the answer. They have to work hard at finding the one big thing but eventually, when they find the answer, they achieve incredible things.

> "They have to work hard at finding the one big thing but eventually, when they find the answer, they achieve incredible things."

It is no use finding the answer to one or two of the questions. You have to answer them all to be able to find your 'one big thing'.

When people or businesses finally identify what they are looking for, they pursue it with relentless determination and focus. How many times are you distracted at work or at home? How easy is it to concentrate on the one big important thing and ignore all the distractions?

It's not easy, and I know that from personal experience. I also know that it really works if you can do it. If you can make an incredible effort to ignore the things that don't really matter and remain focused – almost obsessed – with your quest.

I think that at long last I have found my 'one big thing'. To write, speak and inspire people to change their businesses and lives. Now that I have found my aim in life, it is up to me to go for it and ignore the distractions. I have the belief that I can make it happen, but at the end of the day it is in my own hands.

"I have the belief that I can make it happen, but at the end of the day it is in my own hands."

Try it. Ask yourself the three magic questions, talk about them with your colleagues or friends. Keep going back to them. Keep nagging away at it until you find your 'one big thing'. It won't be easy, and it might take a long time, but I am confident that if you try hard enough you will eventually find it.

"It won't be easy, and it might take a long time, but I am confident that if you try hard enough you will eventually find it."

Don't feed the ducks...

- Be passionate about what you do

- Find your one big thing

- Believe you will achieve it

- Pursue it with relentless determination and focus

- Never give up!

- Make the connection

CHAPTER 23

Sex, Drugs and Rock 'n' Roll

If all else fails,
there is always…

Well, there you have it. Don't feed the ducks… I hope you have been inspired to change your business and create a really successful environment where people are genuinely proud to work.

I hope you have also been inspired to take a positive attitude to life and the many challenges and brilliant experiences it brings.

It can be done, and the great thing is not many people do it. It takes imagination, hard work, determination and, above all, passion. Whatever your goal in life, either at work or at home, you can achieve it if you really believe that you can make things happen.

Sometimes you won't know exactly what you want to achieve with your business or personal ambitions, but personally I think the main thing is that you keep setting yourself goals, targets, things you want to achieve.

You might not know how they are going to end up but one thing is for sure – they will end up somewhere, you will achieve something. I really believe that successful businesses and people are the ones that keep doing things. New things, ambitious things. Look at Richard Branson. He has always pushed himself, tried different projects. He is never afraid to try something fresh and vibrant. Sometimes his projects might fail but he just tries again or moves onto something different.

> "I really believe that
> successful businesses and people
> are the ones that keep doing things.
> New things, ambitious things."

I feel that, without knowing it, my life has always been changing; my aims and goals have constantly been moving. But the key here is, again, that I always have goals – daily, monthly, yearly, formal or informal. On page 188 is what I've called a 'life cartoon' of the major events that have happened in my personal life or at work. I could never have imagined that I would be doing what I am at the moment, speaking, writing and enjoying everything I do.

Notice at the end of the life cartoon there is a big question mark.

That is because I feel my own story is really just starting. I have plans for the future, lots of them, but who knows where they will lead? One thing I will always do is just keep trying, keep moving on.

Why don't you, if you feel like it, do a life diagram of your own, putting down your memories of the important things that have happened to you? You might not be able to draw the pictures but just put down the important words, the things that really mean something to you. It really helped me to look back on it and gain some perspective on life. Try it for yourself, and when you have finished make sure to give yourself five aims for the future, work related or personal, however small or large. Write them down. It is a big step to making them come true.

Finally, one of my best friends, Geoff, told me a true story about a long-winded business meeting he once attended that had been dragging on for hours, seemingly with no real point or focus.

Suddenly, without warning, one of the managers got up out of his seat and boldly proclaimed to his shocked colleagues 'At the end of the day, don't forget all that really matters is sex, drugs and rock and roll!' And with that he walked out of the meeting to a stunned silence.

Whatever your challenges in business or life, whatever your trials and tribulations, remember to have fun. We only have one go at it at the end of the day...

Thanks for reading...

Liam O'Connell
Director of Positivity
Inspirational speaker

Bibliography

Blanchard, K. (2000) *The One Minute Manager*, HarperCollins Business.

Collins, J. (2001) *Good to Great*, Random House Business Books.

McGee, P. (2006) S.U.M.O. *Shut Up, Move On: The Straight Talking Guide to Creating and Enjoying a Brilliant Life*, Capstone Publishing.

Lundin, S., Paul, H. and Christensen, J. (2002) *Fish!: A Remarkable Way to Boost Morale and Improve Results*, Coronet Books.

Seddon, J. (2003) *Freedom from Command and Control*, Vanguard Press.

The Sunday Times 100 Best Companies to Work For, www.timesonline.co.uk/tol/life_and_style/career_and_jobs/best_100_companies

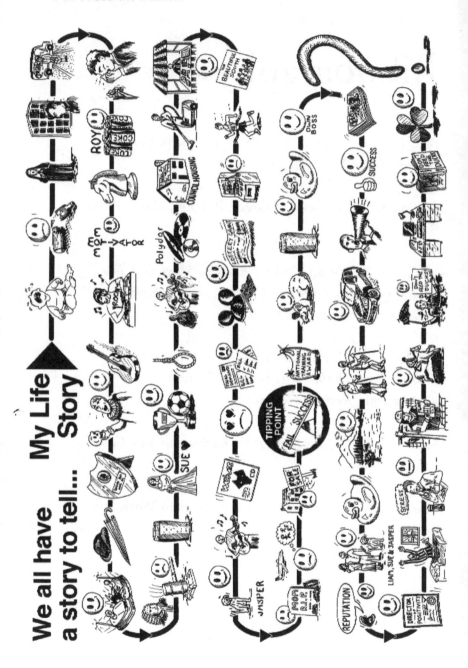

A guide to cultural change and service excellence

Action	Ownership	Percentage completed
1 Understand your baseline position - carry out an employee morale survey. **Happy, focused people = happy customers.** Check current customer service levels.		
2 Agree **target dates** for the cultural change programme.		
3 Create **urgency** and an environment ready for change. There has to be a reason for change. You must appeal to both hearts and minds.		
4 Create a **compelling vision** and set of values to ensure that the vision comes alive within your business.		
5 **Inspire** and **involve** your people at all levels in the change process and in creating the compelling vision and values.		
6 **Obtain buy-in** from your customers and involve them in the process as well.		

Action	Ownership	Percentage completed
7 Ensure the vision and values are **deeply embedded** in every aspect of your business from recruitment, induction processes and employee development.		
8 Create a **strong** visible **internal brand** that mirrors your vision and values and make sure it is displayed everywhere within your business as a constant reminder of your purpose.		
9 Pursue your vision with a **relentless** and determined focus. Lead with passion and commitment. Ensure your managers are fully trained and encouraged to develop their leadership skills.		
10 Surround yourself with **positive people** and recruit for **attitude** and **personality.**		
11 Share a **collective belief** that you will succeed and have **fun** at the same time.		
12 Create a group of **cultural architects** from every area and level of the business and appoint a customer champion to champion the change process.		
13 Take people on regular visits to other **top performing companies** and use their best ideas to improve your business.		

Action	Ownership	Percentage completed
14 Create a robust internal communication culture that **celebrates** every **success** and rewards people appropriately. Think of more imaginative ways than just a wage slip.		
15 Carry out a mystery shopping programme and constantly **test** that **employees** are displaying the right **attitude.**		
16 Carry out an annual employee morale survey and publish the results.		
17 Hold an annual employee conference that is fun, **celebrates success** and **thanks** and **rewards** as many people as possible on the day.		
18 Decide what your **key performance targets** are and display them throughout the business.		
19 Ensure that your **cultural change** and service excellence plan is a regular agenda item and a vital part of management meetings.		

Action	Ownership	Percentage completed
20 **Innovate** and continually involve people in developing new ideas for the business and address current business objectives.		
21 Enter and **win awards** and celebrate every success with your employees. Create a winning mentality. Develop a reputation as **being the best.** Great public relations = higher profile and shared internal success.		
22 **Identify your stars** and retain them at any cost. Encourage any very negative people that the grass might be greener somewhere else.		
23 Go back to step one and **start again**. Cultural change is an ongoing process and only your continued enthusiasm and determination will bring about the success you desire.		